Creating Information in the Header and Footer 39
Using Page Setup 40
Using the Paper Tab 41
Using Print Preview 42
Printing a Document 43
Bullets and Numbering 44
Creating a Bulleted List as you type 44
To Create a Bulleted List from the Bullet Library 44
To Create a Customised Bulleted List 45
Creating a Numbered List 46
To Continue a Numbered List in a Document 46
To Restart Numbering 46
To create your own Numbering Style 47
Exercise 4: - Bulleted Lists 48
Introducing Simple Tables 49
Creating a Table using the Table Grouping Commands 49
Inserting Rows 50
Inserting Columns 50
To Merge or Join Cells in a Table 51
To Delete Rows in a Table 51
To Delete Columns in a Table 51
Creating a Table using the Insert Table Feature 52
Exercise 5: - Creating a Simple Table 54
Section 2: Intermediate Level Objectives 55
Working with Tables 56
Using the AutoFit Feature 56
The AutoFormat Feature 56
To Delete a Table Style 59
Creating a Table using the Drawing Pencil 59
Rotating Text in a Table 60
Exercise 6: - Creating a Booking Form 62
Different Types of Breaks 63
To Create a Section Break 63
To Delete a Page, Column or Section Break 66
Moving between Sections of a Document 66
Exercise 7: - Creating a Header and Footer 67
Identify the Tab Stop Marker 68
Different Tab and Indent Icons 68
Setting Tabs from the Ruler 68
Removing Tabs from the Ruler 69
Setting Tabs using the Tabs Dialog Box 69
Exercise 8: - Creating Tabs using the Tabs Dialog Box 71
What are Styles? 72
How to View Styles in a Document 72
Working with Styles using the Formatting Toolbar 73
To Modify a Style 73
Adding a Style to a Template 75
The Automatically Update Feature 75
Creating a New Style 75
Assigning a Shortcut Key to a New Style 76

Deleting a Style already added to a Template 78
Exercise 9: - Creating a Document using Styles 80
Bookmarks 81
To Add a Bookmark 81
To Locate a Bookmark 82
To Delete a Bookmark 83
Creating a Table of Contents 83
Exercise 10: - Updating a Table of Contents 85
Indexes 86
Creating an Index 86
AutoSummarise 89
To Read a Summary of an Online Document 89
To Alter the Display of a Document 90
Display or Highlight Key Points in a Document 90
To Delete a Summary 90
Reviewing a Document using Track Changes 91
How to use Track Changes 91
Using Comments 92
To Insert a Comment 92
To Edit a Comment 92
To View Comments 93
To Delete a Comment 93
To Compare and Combine Multiple Copies of a Document 93
Mail Merge 96
Creating Letters using Mail Merge 96
Creating Labels using Mail Merge 106
Exercise 11: - Creating Labels 113
Templates 114
To Save a Document as a Template 114
View a Template 115
Open and Amend an Existing Template 116
Section 3: Expert Level Objectives 118
Using Outline View 119
The Outline Commands 119
Outlining an Existing Document 119
Promote and Demote Information 120
Move Information in Outline View 121
Exercise 12: - Working with a Table of Contents 122
Create an Outlined Numbered List 123
Master Documents 124
Creating a Master Document 124
Opening a Subdocument 125
Inserting a Subdocument 125
Moving a Subdocument 126
Delete a Subdocument 127
Lock and Unlock Subdocuments 127
Using the Form Commands 127
Exercise 13: - Creating a Form using the Form Commands 128
Inserting Text Form Fields 129
Inserting Check Box Form Fields 129

Customising the Text Form Fields 130
Customising the Check Box Form Fields 132
Protecting Forms 134
Define AutoText Entries 136
Create Date Fields 138
Using the AutoText List 139
Using the ASK Field 140
Exercise 14: - Using Fill-in Fields 142
Macros 144
Record a Macro 144
Assigning a Macro to a Shortcut Key 146
Using the Menu Bar to View and Edit a Macro 147
Deleting a Macro 149
Exercise 15: - Generate a Table of Contents Macro 150
Watermarks 151
Picture Watermarks 151
Creating a Text Watermark 152
To Customise a Text Watermark 152
To Delete a Watermark 153
Exercise 16: - Creating a Watermark 154
Hyperlinks 155
Creating a Hyperlink to an Internet Address 155
Creating a Hyperlink in a Document 156
Edit a Hyperlink 157
Delete a Hyperlink 157
Using Format Columns Feature 158
Insert a Chart in a Document 160
Edit a Chart 161
Copy Information from Excel 161
Using Edit Paste Special 162
Exercise 17: - Using Columns, Hyperlinks and Macros 163
Working with Graphics 164
Inserting a Picture in a Document 164
Edit a Picture in a Document 165
Cropping Pictures 166
Inserting WordArt into a Document 168
To add a shadow 170
Edit WordArt in a Document 170
Format WordArt in a Document 170
Adding AutoShapes to Documents 171
Using the Drawing Toolbar 172
To Draw Objects from a Central Point 173
Using Text Boxes 174
To Link a Text Box 174
Display Text Box Tools 175
To use Text Wrapping 175
Using Footnotes and Endnotes 177
Inserting a Footnote 177
Inserting a Endnote 177
To Amend a Footnote or Endnote 178

To Delete a Footnote or Endnote 178
To Start Renumbering a Footnote or Endnote 178
Shortcut Keys 179
Notes Pages 180
Index 181

Section 1: Foundation Level Objectives

- Introduction to Word
- Tour of the Screen
- Creating New Documents
- Opening and Saving Documents
- Using Spell and Grammar Features
- Format Options Font and Paragraph
- Creating Header and Footer Information
- Using Portrait and Landscape Features
- Print Preview and Printing Options
- Inserting Bullets and Numbering
- Introduction to Simple Tables

Note: If you are working in Windows XP instead of Windows Vista, dialog boxes may look different but function in a similar way.

Introducing the Word Screen

Word 2007 is a word processing application that runs in a Windows environment allowing you to create and edit professional-looking documents fast and easy. Its user-friendly prompts help to identify icons on the screen that you maybe unfamiliar with and takes you through the various functions within this application.

Tour of the Screen

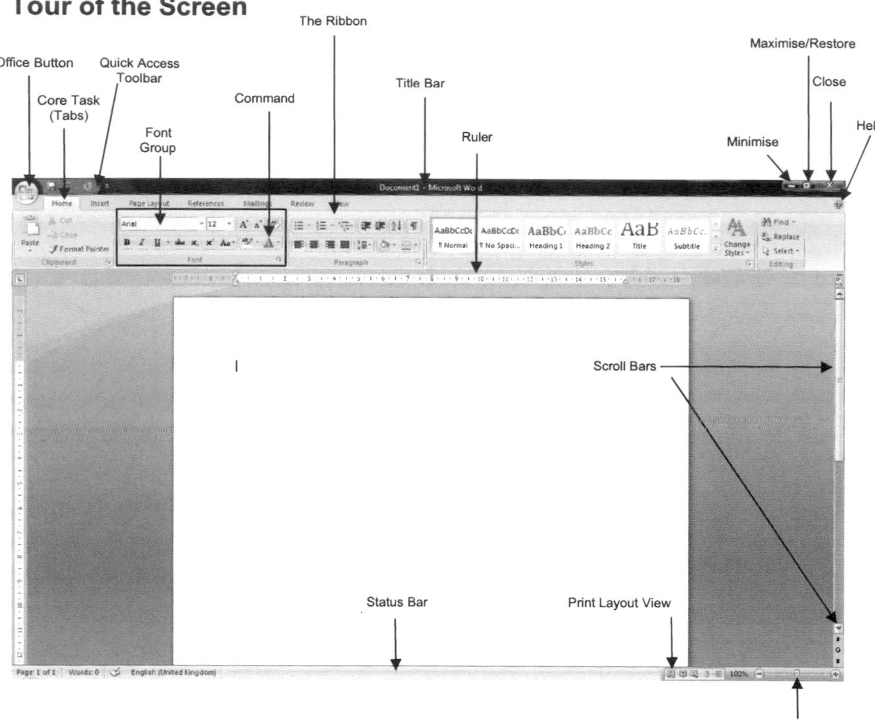

Figure 1

Office Button

In Word 2007 the Office Button replaces the file menu found in previous versions of Word and displays the commands for New, Open, Convert, Save, Save As, Print, Prepare, Send, Publish, Business Contact Manager and Close and the related options available under each command.

Quick Access Toolbar

The Quick Access Toolbar can be found in the top section of the screen. It allows the user to display commands that are regularly used and that are independent of their associated tabs. There is the option to locate the Quick Access Toolbar in two locations near to the top section of the screen.

Title Bar

The Title Bar is highlighted at the top of the screen and defines the programme that you are in and the name of the Word document that you have opened. MS Word will automatically display the default name, for example Document1, however once the document has been saved the name of the saved document will be displayed in this area.

The Ribbon

The Ribbon is new to Word 2007 and is the control centre to quickly help you find the commands that help you complete a task. The Ribbon is organised into three parts

1. **Core Tasks:** consisting of seven Tabs

   Home, Insert, Page Layout, References, Mailings, Review and View

2. **Groups:** related items grouped together
3. **Commands:** buttons, boxes and menus that give instruction

The Ribbon organises the commands into logical groups all collected together under the Tabs with each Tab relating to a type of activity. Some Tabs only appear when they are needed whilst others are visible all the time.

To minimise the Ribbon double click with the left button on the active Tab, for example Home, the Ribbon and its commands disappear. To display the Ribbon and its commands, click with the left button on the Tab. Alternatively press Ctrl F1 to collapse or expand the tabs.

Help

The Help icon can be found on the Ribbon or by pressing F1

Ruler

When working in Print Layout, Web Layout or Draft View options, a horizontal ruler is displayed as a default. A vertical ruler can also be viewed in Print Layout View and Print Preview.

Scroll Bars

Horizontal and Vertical scroll bars enable users to move around the document.

Zoom Control

To use the Zoom Control drag with the left button to increase (magnify) or decrease the worksheet to display the information larger or smaller on screen.

Status Bar

The Status Bar is at the bottom of the screen, to customise the Status Bar

1. Right click on the Status Bar, the Customise Status Bar appears
2. To activate Caps Lock to be displayed in the Status Bar
3. Click with the left button on Caps Lock
4. A tick is displayed to indicate the feature has been activated
5. Click back in the worksheet
6. Press the Caps key on the keyboard
7. Caps Lock is displayed in the Status Bar to show that it is activated
8. Click the Caps key on the keyboard a second time to switch the feature off

The Status Bar at the bottom of the screen displays the page, section and the total number of pages in a document.

Print Layout View

Print Layout View is useful to see graphics; it provides a fast and easy way for editing information in the Header and Footer.

Full Screen Reading View

The Full Screen Reading View allows the user to hide all toolbars except for the reading layout and reviewing toolbars enabling the user to read the text more easily.

Web Layout View

The Web Layout View is useful when creating a web page or to review a web based document on screen. This icon allows you to see how features are positioned in web page view.

Outline View

The Outline View allows you to look at the structure of a document; it also collapses a document so you see only the main headings.

Draft View

The Draft View can be found at the bottom right hand side of the screen and has replaced Normal View that was available in previous versions of Word.

Opening Microsoft Word

There are several ways that this application can be opened. To open the Word 2007 application, select the Start Button, move the mouse pointer and pause over All Programs, click with the left button on Microsoft Office; select Microsoft Office Word 2007, click with the left button to open the programme.

Working with Drives, Folders and Files

How Information is stored on the Computer

Information is stored on a computer to make it easy for the user to find by organising the information into three levels using Drives, Folders and Files.

A Drive is a physical storage device for holding folders and files. The (C:) drive is the hard disk, other drives may include for example, depending on the specification of the computer, the (A:) drive - the floppy disk, a CD-ROM drive, DVD RW and a USB port that allows information to be stored on a portable USB device. If the computer is on a network you may be able to access the hard drive of other computers via the network drive.

A Folder is the container for the files that are grouped into folders that are easier to find and work with and can be broken down into sub folders. A folder may contain thousands of files.

A File is the computer's basic unit for information storage. Everything on a computer is stored in a file of one type or another.

Figure 2

Documents

Documents is a folder that provides you with a convenient place to store documents, graphics, or other files you want to access quickly. When you save a file in a program such as Word, the file is automatically saved in Documents, unless you choose a different folder. This is normally your personal drive and displays the folders and files that you work with on a regular basis.

Creating a Folder

1. Select Start , Documents to display the Documents area
2. Click with the left button on Organize
3. Choose Layout , Menu Bar
4. The Menu Bar is displayed File Edit View Tools Help
5. Select File, New , Folder
6. The New Folder appears in the right hand pane highlighted in blue
7. Type Introduction to 2007 in the highlighted area
8. Press Enter, to display the Introduction to 2007 folder

Creating a Sub-Folder

1. Double click the left button to open the Introduction to 2007 folder
2. Select File, New , Folder
3. Create a new folder, named Microsoft Excel, press Enter to display the folder
4. Repeat the process to create sub folders for Microsoft PowerPoint and Microsoft Word
5. To change a folder's name, right click on the folder Microsoft Word
6. Choose Rename to highlight the folder
7. Rename the folder as Microsoft Word 2007, press Enter

Creating and Saving a Document

When you start to type text within a document, you will notice a flashing cursor seen as a vertical black line. This flashes and indicates the point at which you will start typing. As you type the text starts to appear from left to right.

When typing if you want to move back a few characters you can either, move on the screen by holding down the left button and moving the cursor, or use the ← key on your keyboard.

Text moves down the screen as you create your document. The space bar on the keyboard is used to create a space between words. Capitalisation is achieved by using the Caps Lock icon Caps on the keyboard. Reselect Caps to switch back to lowercase. To capitalise one character at a time, move the cursor to the character you want to capitalise, hold the Shift key down, select the letter that you want to appear as a capital and let go of the Shift key to continue typing in lowercase.

1. To open a new blank document, select the Office Button
2. Select New with the left button
3. Double click with the left button on Blank document
4. Alternatively select Blank and recent, press Create
5. The new blank document appears
6. Type in the document "My First Document"
7. Select the Office Button ,choose Save As
8. The Save As dialog box appears

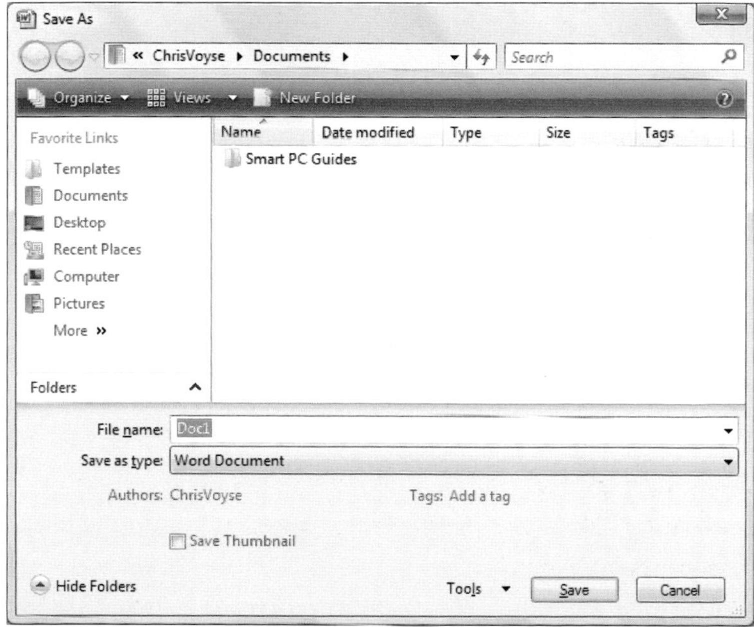

Figure 3

9. In the File name box type Creating My First Document in Word
10. The Save as type area defaults as a Word Document

11. Select Save

12. The Title Bar area at the top of the screen now displays the named document as Creating My First Document in Word - Microsoft Word

13. Alternatively press F12 to display the Save As dialog box

Note: If the document was to be saved to a different drive for example the DVD-RW Drive**, choose** Computer **from the Favourite Links area and select the appropriate drive to save the document.**

Exercise 1: - Creating and Saving a Document in Word

IS IT SCIENCE?

You either love it or hate it! Whatever you feel gardening is the perfect way to wheel away the stresses of the day.

Once you have grasped how a plant works you are in a position to bend it to your will. There are not many plants in the garden that can be left entirely to their own devices and the right time to do a job in the garden is when you have the time to do it properly.

Pruning is the removal of stems, branches or roots of a tree or shrub in order to alter the shape of the plant, to increase vigour or remove dead or damaged parts. It also helps to improve the quality and quantity of flowers and fruits.

Dead heading is one sort of summer pruning we can do that not only keeps the plant tidy but it encourages a new growth of flowers within days.

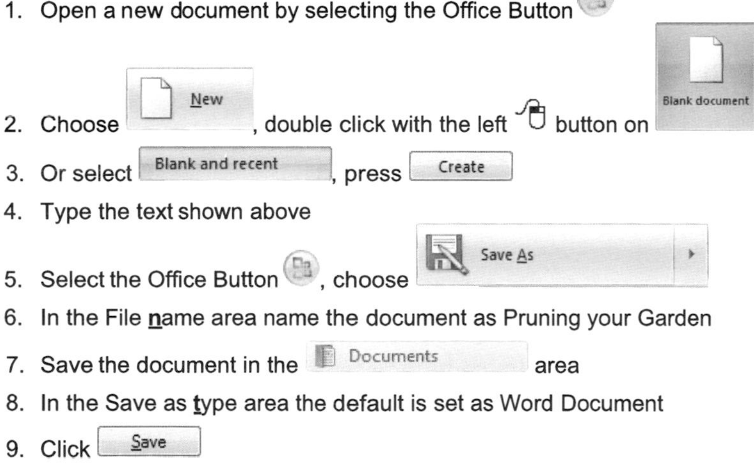

1. Open a new document by selecting the Office Button
2. Choose New, double click with the left button on Blank document
3. Or select Blank and recent, press Create
4. Type the text shown above
5. Select the Office Button, choose Save As
6. In the File name area name the document as Pruning your Garden
7. Save the document in the Documents area
8. In the Save as type area the default is set as Word Document
9. Click Save

Opening Documents using the Office Button

1. Click on the Office Button
2. The Recent Documents area displays the latest documents used
3. Click with the left button on the required document
4. Or use the keyboard by holding down the Alt key, press the letter F
5. Use the → or ↓ arrow keys to highlight the file
6. Press the Enter key to open the document

Opening a Document using the Mouse

1. Press the Office Button, click Open...
2. The Open dialog box appears

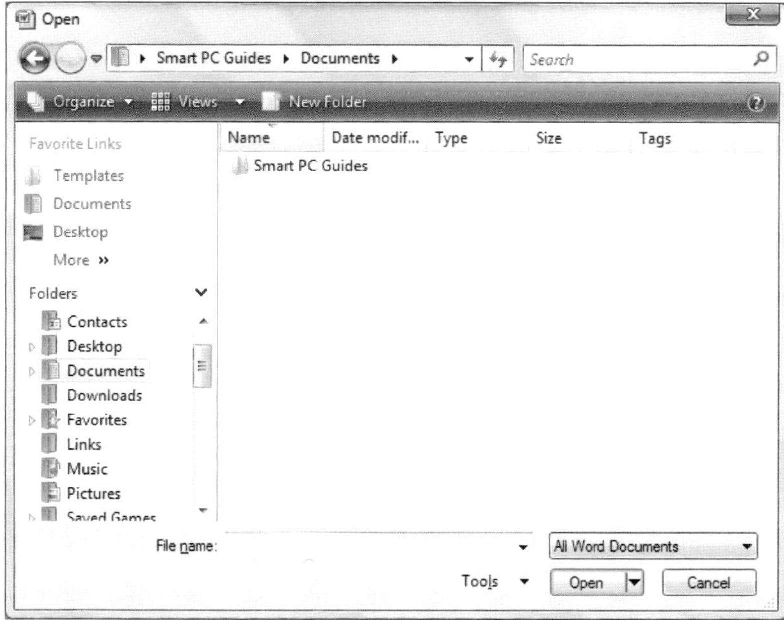

Figure 4

3. Choose Documents or the drive that contains the document
4. Double click with the left button to open the required folder
5. Or click the left button on the individual document, press Open

Opening Several Documents using the Control Key

1. Press the Office Button ,click Open...
2. Choose Documents from Favourite Links area
3. Double click on the required folder to display the list of documents
4. Click the filename once with the left button to select the first document
5. Hold the Ctrl key down to select the next documents
6. Each selected file is highlighted in blue
7. If a file is selected by mistake click again to deselect
8. Click Open to open all the Word documents

Opening Several Workbooks using the Shift Key

1. Press the Office Button ,click Open...
2. Choose Documents from Favourite Links area
3. Double click on the required folder to display the list of documents
4. Click the left button to select the first document
5. Hold the Shift key down, click the left button to select the last document
6. All selected files are highlighted in blue
7. Click Open to display all the documents

Amending or Deleting recently used Files

1. Choose the Office Button
2. Select Word Options, Advanced
3. The Word Options dialog box appears
4. Choose the option Display
5. Select the Number of document in the Recent Documents list:

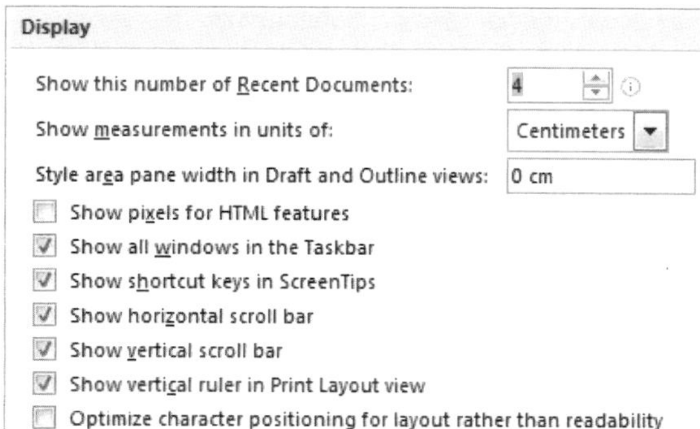

Figure 5

6. Type in the number 10, click OK
7. To activate the new defaults, click the Office Button 
8. Select New, choose Create

Using the Spell and Grammar Facility

The Spell and Grammar feature checks the text in a document for incorrect spelling and grammatical errors using the standard built in dictionary that can also be customised. If an item has been miss spelt the item has a red underline whilst grammatical errors have green underline.

1. Select the Review Tab, choose Spelling & Grammar, alternatively press F7
2. The Spelling and Grammar dialog box appears if there are spelling errors in the text that are not in the dictionary

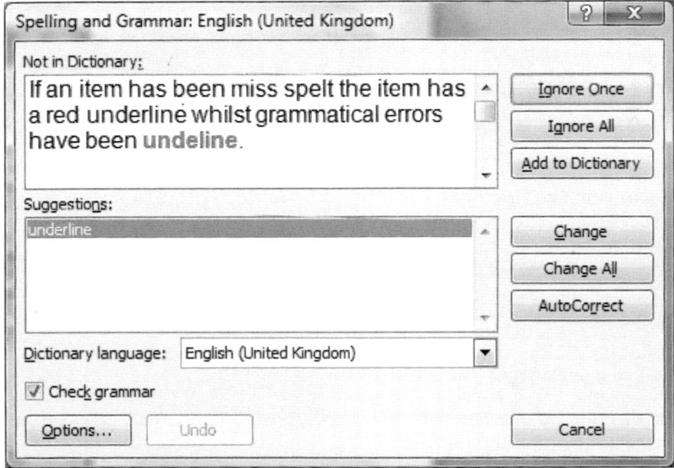

Figure 6

3. The suggestio**n**s area gives alternative spellings
4. Choose the correct spelling, click Change to replace the word
5. The spelling and grammar facility continues to the end of the document
6. Once the spell check has been completed the following dialog box appears

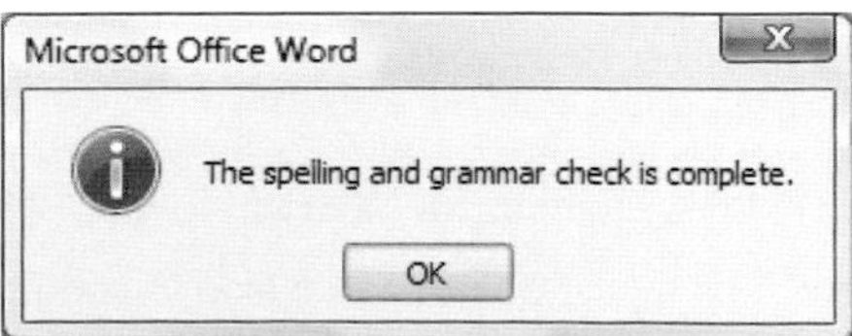

Figure 7

7. Press OK

Adding Words to the Dictionary

1. To add a word to the dictionary, for example a company name
2. Click Add to Dictionary in the spell checker dialog box
3. Press OK

Grammar Check Facility

1. Grammatical errors are highlighted where alternative suggestions are given

Figure 8

2. The grammatical checker offers the option to ignore once, ignore rule or change the grammatical error

Using the Undo and Redo Facility

When text is entered in a document that information is stored in the memory. The Undo and Redo facility allows you to either go backwards or forwards on a step by step basis. The Undo and Redo icons can be found on the Quick Access Toolbar located at the top of the screen.

1. To undo an action click on the Undo icon
2. Repeat the same steps for the Redo icon
3. Alternatively press Ctrl Z to undo changes, or Ctrl Y to redo changes
4. Click on the downward arrow on the Undo and Redo icon to undo or redo a series of changes

Note: If you clicked on the downward arrow and selected the stage that you want to go back to it will delete all the steps.

Highlighting Information in a Document

Highlighting a Character, Word, Paragraph or Document

Before you can change the appearance of text, the text has to be highlighted.

Highlight by Characters

1. Position the cursor in front of the character you want to highlight
2. Hold down the Shift key, press the arrow →
3. Each character is highlighted in blue

Highlight a Word

1. Position the cursor over the word you want to highlight
2. Double click with the left button on the word
3. The word is highlighted in blue
4. Or place the cursor at the front of the word you want to highlight, hold down the left button
5. Drag along the word, the word is highlighted in blue

Highlight a Sentence

1. Position the cursor anywhere in the sentence you want to highlight
2. Hold the Ctrl key down
3. Click the left button anywhere in the sentence
4. The sentence is highlighted in blue

Highlight a Paragraph

1. Position the cursor anywhere in the paragraph you want to highlight
2. Click with the left button three times in the middle of the paragraph
3. Or move the cursor to the left hand margin, a white arrow appears, click twice to highlight the area
4. The paragraph is highlighted in blue

Highlight the Whole Document

1. Hold down the Ctrl key, press A the document is highlighted in blue

Moving Information in a Document

1. Highlight the information to be moved
2. Select Home, click on the Cut icon in the Clipboard Grouping
3. The information disappears and moves to the clipboard
4. Using the left button, click where you want the information to appear
5. Select the Paste icon Paste from the Clipboard Grouping

Using the Mouse to Move Information

1. Double click in a word to highlight a word
2. Hold down the left button, right click, select Cut
3. The information disappears and moves to the clipboard
4. Using the left button, click where you want the information to appear
5. Hold down the right button, select Paste
6. The information appears from the clipboard into the selected area

Using Keyboard Shortcuts to Move Information

1. Select the word by double clicking in the middle of the word
2. Hold down the Ctrl key, select X
3. The information disappears and moves to the clipboard
4. Using the left button, click where you want the information to appear
5. Hold down the Ctrl key, select V
6. The information appears from the clipboard into the selected area

Using the Mouse Pointer to Move, Drag and Drop Information

1. Double click in a word to highlight the word
2. Move the mouse pointer over the highlighted word
3. Click and hold down the left button
4. Move to where? appears in the bottom left hand corner of the Status Bar
5. Drag to the new location with the mouse pointer , let go of the mouse
6. The information appears in the selected area

Note: This is a useful way to move information over small distances.

Copying Information in a Document

1. Highlight the information you want to copy
2. Select Home, choose the Copy icon
3. Click with your left button where the information will be inserted
4. Select 

Using the Mouse to Copy Information

1. Double click in a word to highlight a word
2. Hold down the left button, select Copy
3. The information disappears and moves to the clipboard
4. Using the left button, click where you want the information to appear
5. Press the right button, select Paste
6. The information appears from the clipboard into the selected area

Using Keyboard Shortcuts to Copy Information

1. Select the word by double clicking in the middle of the word
2. Press the Ctrl key, select C, information is copied to the clipboard
3. Click with your left button where the information will be inserted
4. Hold down the Ctrl key, select V
5. The information is copied from the clipboard into the selected area

Using the Mouse Pointer to Drag and Copy Information

1. Double click in a word to highlight a word
2. Move your mouse pointer over the highlighted word
3. Hold down the Ctrl key and the left button
4. Copy to where? appears in the bottom left hand corner of the status bar
5. Drag to the new location with the mouse pointer
6. Release the left button before the Ctrl key
7. The selected information has been copied

Exercise 2: - Using the Copy and Move Functions

The Role of IT Today

The role of information technology has been steadily increasing in importance during recent times. The forward thinking business runs best with the help of modern technology, technology that improves productivity and implements cost-effective business solutions. Powerful desktop microcomputers, which are one application of this technology, can be used for a variety of purposes some of which are listed below:

Preparing and presenting reports by means of word processors

Manipulating large data sets by fact-using disciplines

Analysing complex texts

Developing innovative art forms, both visual and sound

Accessing texts, graphics and data via the internet

Developing valuable keyboard skills

Whatever the area of business, the Role of IT can serve to improve business communications and make life easier for everyone.

1. Open a new blank document
2. Type the text shown in Exercise 2 shown above
3. Highlight a sentence and move it to the end of the document
4. Highlight a word and copy to a destination of your choice
5. Spell check the document
6. Save the document as Using the Copy and Move Functions

Smart Tags

A Smart Tag is an indicator that appears at different times when working in Word. The Smart Tags button when selected allows the user to perform a variety of tasks such as sending mail by opening up a new mail message dialog window, schedule a meeting, open an existing persons contact details, add a new contact or insert an address into the document. To view if the smart tag facility is switched on.

1. Select the Office Button, choose Word Options, Proofing
2. Alternatively press Alt F I P
3. Choose AutoCorrect Options..., or press Alt A
4. Select Smart Tags
5. Complete the Smart Tags dialog box as shown below

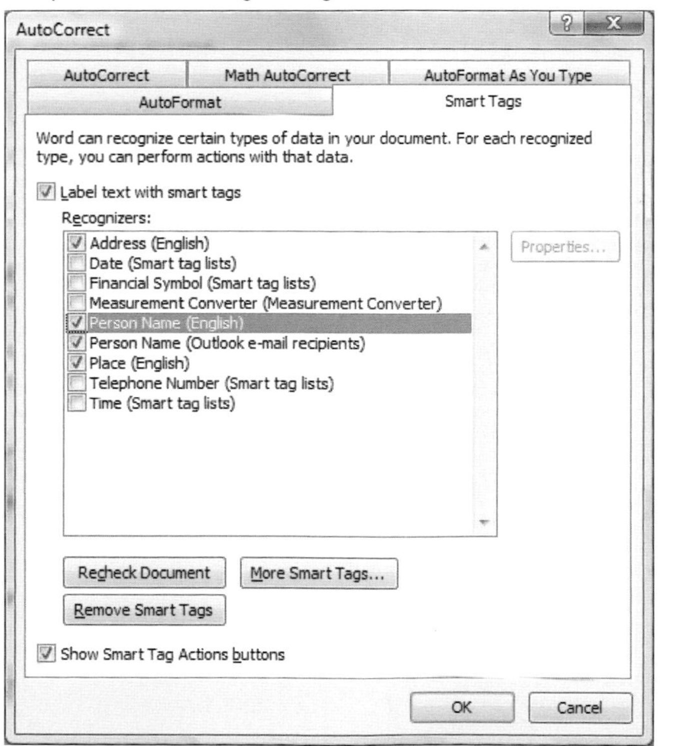

Figure 9

6. Press OK twice

7. Type your first name and surname in the document
8. Press Enter, move the mouse pointer over your name
9. A Smart Tag Indicator appears

Removing a Smart Tag

1. Select the Smart Tag
2. Click on the Smart Tag icon to extend the menu box

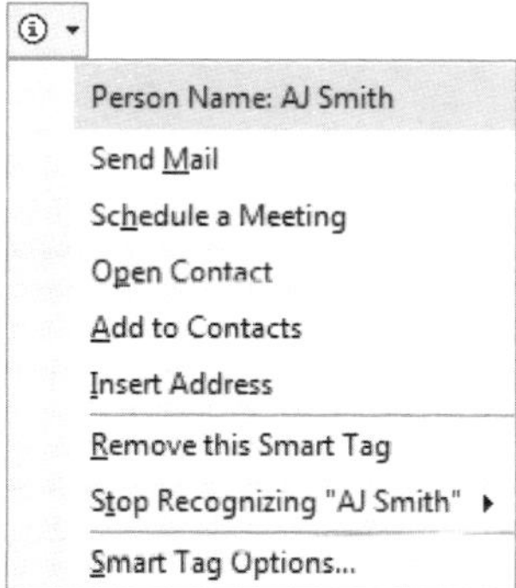

Figure 10

3. Select Remove this Smart Tag

Note: **Smart Tags are not recognised if there is a spelling error or a name, for example a personal or company name that has not been already added to the dictionary.**

Exercise 3: - Using Smart Tags to Add an Address

1. Open a new document
2. Type your first name and surname, press Enter
3. Move the mouse pointer over your name
4. Select the Smart Tag icon, choose Add to Contacts
5. Complete the Address Details
6. Save and close to update the Contact Information
7. Reselect the Smart Tag icon, choose Insert Address
8. The address appears in the document

Hard Spaces

To ensure that names of individuals or organisations stay together, a hard space can to be created.

Creating a Hard Space

1. Select Home
2. Click on the Show/Hide icon ¶ from the Paragraph Grouping
3. Type out the name SMART
4. Hold down the Ctrl and Shift keys and press the spacebar
5. Type out the name Guides
6. A hard space is shown as a degree sign between the two words SMART°Guides¶

Using the AutoCorrect Feature

The AutoCorrect feature corrects miss spelt words automatically.

To Open the AutoCorrect Facility

1. Select the Office Button, choose Word Options, Proofing
2. Alternatively press Alt F I P
3. Choose AutoCorrect Options..., or press Alt A
4. Ensure the AutoCorrect Tab is selected

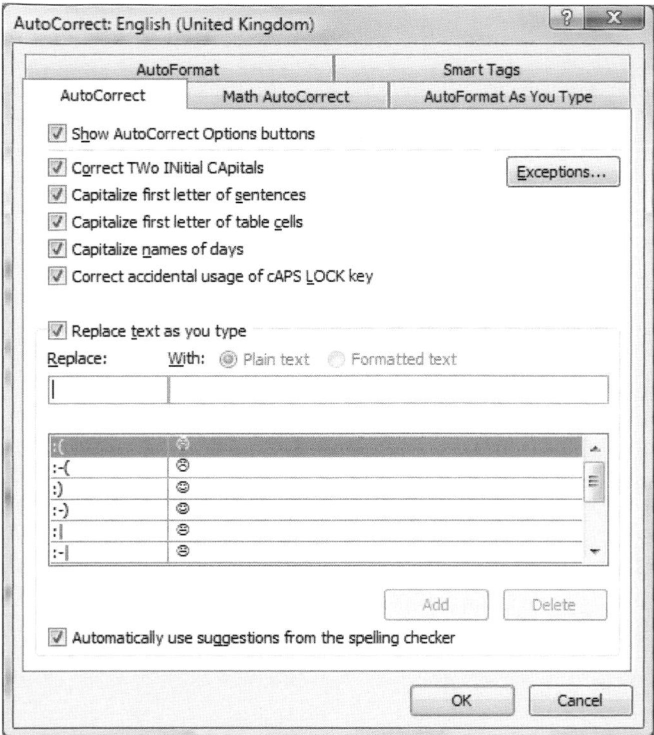

Figure 11

5. Type out sg in the **R**eplace box as shown below

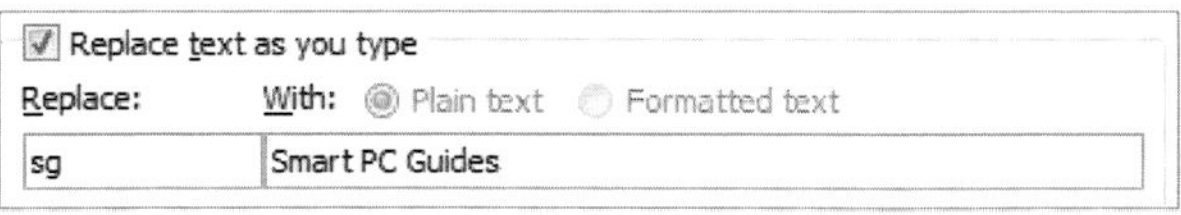

Figure 12

6. In the **W**ith box type Smart PC Guides
7. Select [Add], click [OK]
8. Click [OK] to exit the Word Options dialog box
9. Open a new document
10. Type sg (in lowercase) press the spacebar
11. The text Smart PC Guides appears
12. Type SG (in uppercase) press the spacebar
13. Smart PC Guides appears

Note: If the abbreviation in the replace box was defined in uppercase it would only appear in a document if the abbreviation was typed in uppercase.

Deleting an AutoCorrect Entry

1. Select the Office Button, choose Word Options, Proofing
2. Alternatively press Alt F I P
3. Choose AutoCorrect Options..., or press Alt A
4. Ensure the AutoCorrect Tab is selected
5. In The Replace box, type the abbreviation you want to delete
6. The abbreviation appears at the top of the list underneath the Replace box
7. Press Delete click OK twice

Format Options

Formatting allows you to change the appearance of documents and to maintain consistency throughout documents. Formatting is quick and easy using the predesigned themes or you can customise documents to suit your own requirements.

The Font Group Icons

Icon	Shortcut Keys	Descriptive Prompt
Arial	Ctrl Shift F	Font Face
10	Ctrl Shift P	Font Size
A	Ctrl Shift >	Increase Font Size
A	Ctrl Shift <	Decrease Font Size
	Alt H E	Clear all the Formatting from selected area
B	Ctrl B	Makes selected text and numbers bold
I	Ctrl I	Makes selected text and numbers italic
U	Ctrl U	Underlines selected text and numbers
abc	Alt H 4	Draws a line through middle of text
x_2	Ctrl =	Subscript: Creates small letters below line of text
x^2	Ctrl Shift +	Superscript: Creates small letters above line of text
Aa		Changes text to uppercase, lowercase or titlecase
ab		Makes text look like it's marked with a highlighter pen
A		Change Font Colour

Figure 13

Formatting using the Font Group

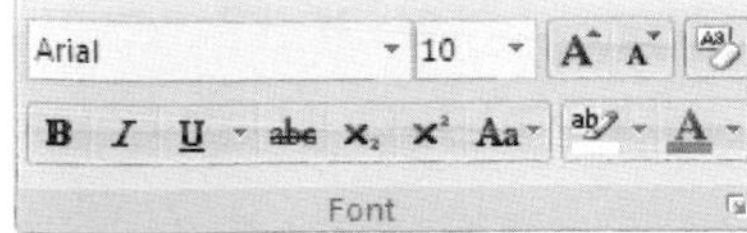

Figure 14

1. Open an existing document and highlight the text you want to change
2. Click on the Font Face icon Arial
3. Using the downward arrow, change the font to Calibri (Body)
4. Click on the Font Size icon 10
5. Using the downward arrow change the font size to 14
6. Click on the Font Colour icon
7. Using the downward arrow, choose a different colour

The Highlight icon marks text to make it stand out in a document.

1. Select the colour of highlight by clicking on the downward arrow
2. Select the text you want to highlight
3. Click on the Highlight icon to switch off the highlight facility

Formatting using the Menu Options

1. Select the text you want to format, click with the right button
2. Choose Font..., the Font dialog box appears

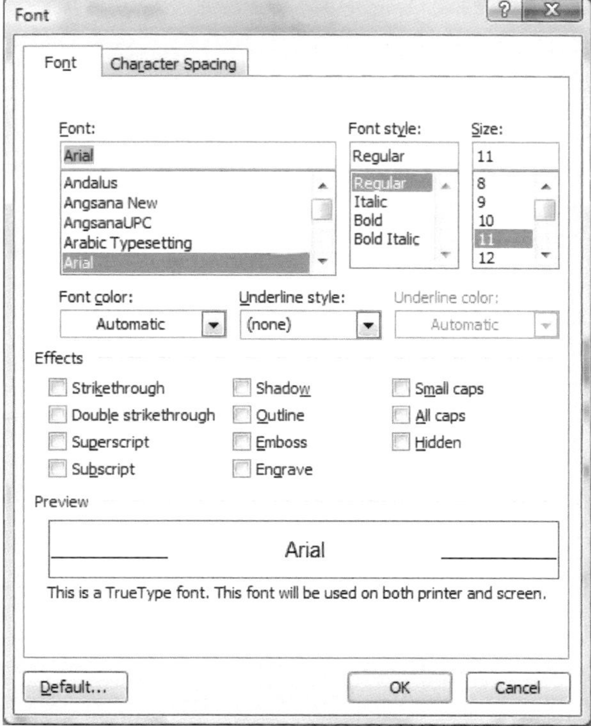

Figure 15

3. Use the downward arrows to select your options
4. The preview area displays how the changes will look
5. Confirm changes and return to the document by selecting OK

The Paragraph Group Icons

Icon		Descriptive Prompt
	Ctrl L	Aligns text, numbers or inline objects to the left
	Ctrl E	Centres text, numbers or inline objects
	Ctrl R	Aligns text, numbers or inline objects to the right
	Ctrl J	Aligns text to both the left and right margins
	Alt H K	Changes spacing between lines of text
	Alt H H	Colour the background behind text
	Alt H B	Customise borders of selected text
	Alt H U	Start a bulleted list
	Alt H N	Start a numbered list
	Alt H M	Start a multilevel list
		Decrease the indent level of the paragraph
		Increase the indent level of the paragraph
	Alt H S O	Sort alphabetically
¶	Alt H 8	Show paragraph marks and hidden formatting symbols
	Ctrl D	Displays Font dialog box

Figure 16

Formatting using the Paragraph Group

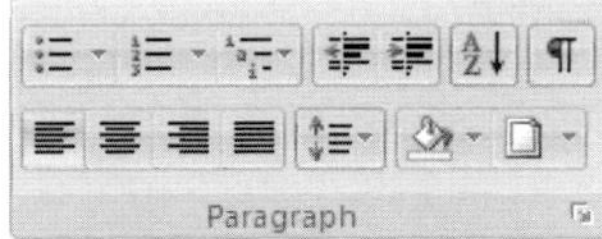

Figure 17

1. Highlight a paragraph to be changed
2. Click with the right button, choose Paragraph...
3. The Paragraph dialog box appear

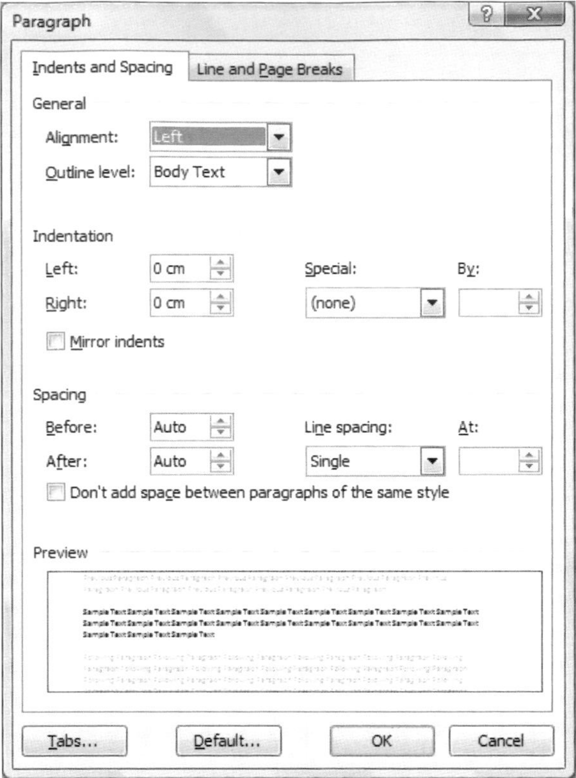

Figure 18

4. The Alignment Box displays the alignment used in the original paragraph
5. To change this option click on the downward pointing arrow
6. Choose the required alignment
7. The preview area displays the amended paragraph
8. The Indentation Box allows the user to change the indentation of the text

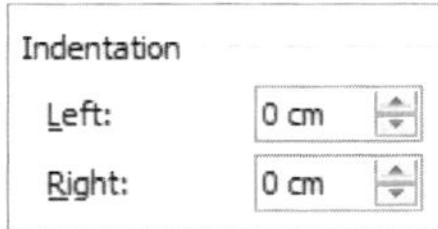

Figure 19

9. Select the arrows and choose the indentation required
10. Preview displays the position of the changed paragraph

11. The **S**pecial Feature Box allows the user to create different Indents

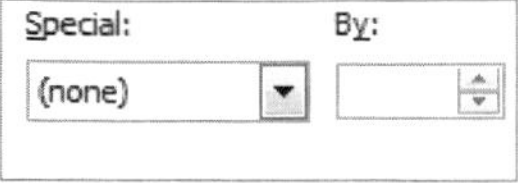

Figure 20

12. Select First Line Indent, the preview area displays the style of indent
13. Choose Hanging Indent
14. To accept any changes, click OK
15. The Line and **P**age Breaks Tab covers the following options

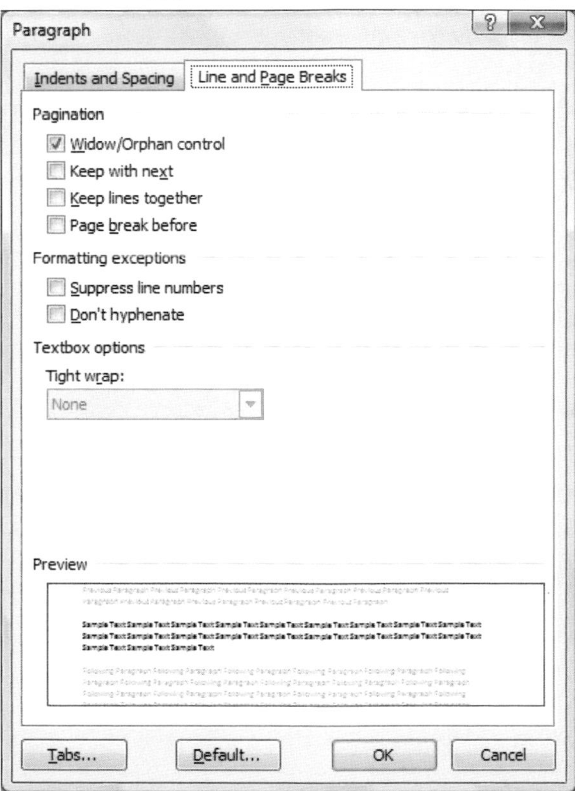

Figure 21

Widow/Orphan Control

The Widow Control sends a single sentence to the next page leaving the remainder of the paragraph on the previous page. Orphan Control leaves sentences while the rest of the text is on the next page. The default is to switch the **W**idow/Orphan control on.

Keep Lines Together

If a paragraph is highlighted using the Keep lines together option the paragraph will not be split up by a page break.

Keep with Next Option

The Keep with next option keeps highlighted paragraphs together.

Page Break Before

Page break before is normally applied to headings to force the page break before a selected paragraph.

Suppress Line Numbers

Suppress line numbers prevents line numbers from appearing next to selected paragraphs where line numbers have been set.

Text Wrap

Text wrap allows text to be wrapped around pictures, shapes and tables, choosing any style or position required.

Using the Format Painter

Using the Format Painter icon allows users to copy formatting from one place and apply it to another.

1. Select the text to be copied
2. Choose the Home Tab
3. Move the mouse pointer to the Format Painter icon Format Painter
4. Double click on Format Painter to copy the format
5. When the Format Painter icon is switched on it is displayed in orange
6. Click with the left button on the text you want to copy the format to
7. The text is changed to match the selected format
8. Switch Format Painter off by selecting the icon again

Header and Footer Information

Headers and Footers in a document allow the user to insert text that appears at the top or bottom of every page. The header and footer groupings can be found under the Insert Tab.

Figure 22

Creating Information in the Header and Footer

To create information in the header and footer, for example a company name or page numbers

1. Open a document, select Insert
2. Choose Header from the Header and Footer Group, select Edit Header
3. The header box appears at the top of your document
4. Type Smart PC Guides next to the flashing cursor

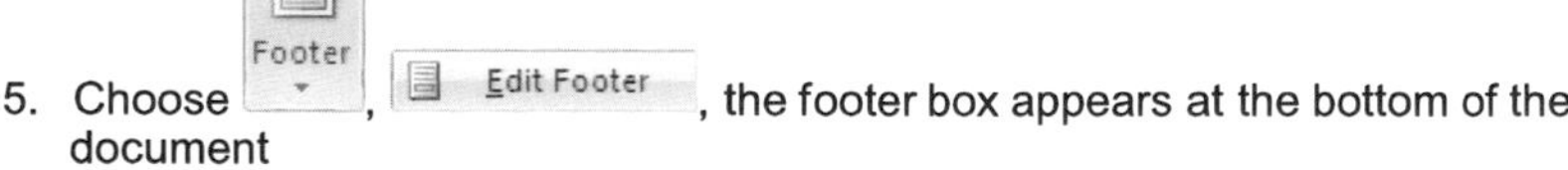

5. Choose Footer, Edit Footer, the footer box appears at the bottom of the document
6. Type your first and second name next to the flashing cursor
7. Press Tab on the keyboard to move to the centre of the footer

8. Select Page Number, Bottom of Page to expand the menu
9. Using the downward arrow key, choose Page X of Y

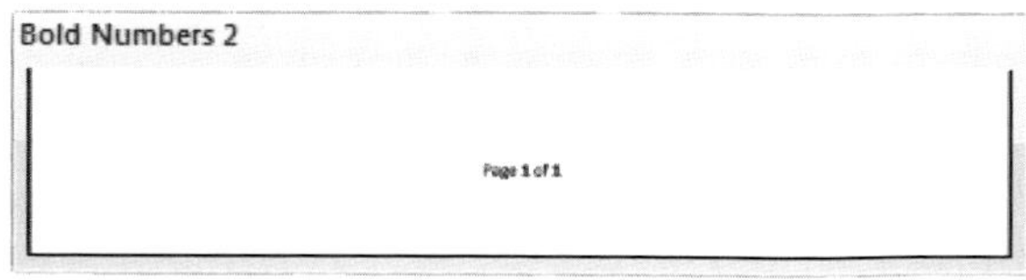

Figure 23

10. The page number appears at the foot of the page

Using Page Setup

The Page Setup Group is found under the Page Layout Tab and enables a user to define the Margins, Paper and Layout of a document.

1. Click on the Page Layout Tab, choose Margins from the Page Setup Group
2. Select Custom Margins..., the Page Setup dialog box appears

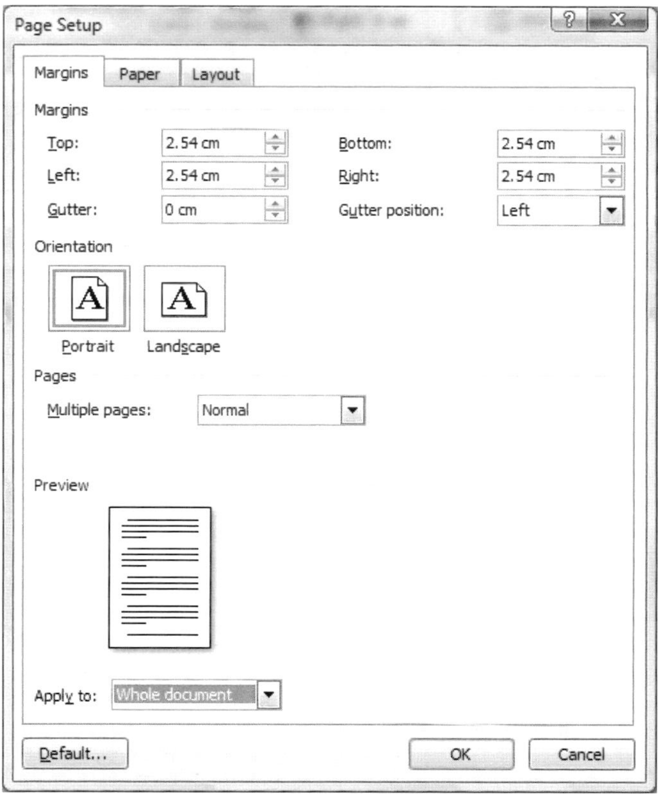

Figure 24

3. Use the arrow keys to change the default margins <u>T</u>op, <u>B</u>ottom, <u>L</u>eft, <u>Ri</u>ght and <u>G</u>utter as required
4. The <u>G</u>utter margin facility creates extra space when binding documents
5. Change the page layout by selecting Portrait or Landscape
6. Press the downward arrow in the Appl<u>y</u> to area
7. Select this point forward or the whole document, click OK

Using the Paper Tab

The Paper Tab allows the user to set the paper size or define a custom style.

1. Click on the Page Layout Tab, choose Size from the Page Setup Group
2. Select More Paper Sizes..., the Page Setup dialog box appears

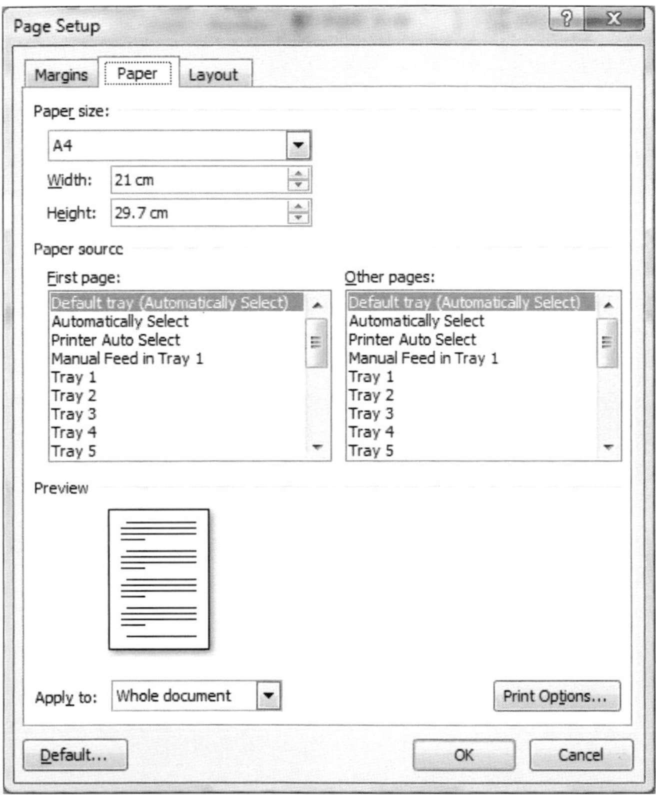

Figure 25

3. Select the required Paper size using the downward arrow
4. The Apply to area enables the user to select whether the amended features relate to this section, this point forward or the whole document
5. Click OK

Using Print Preview

Print Preview lets the user view a document to see how the finished document looks before printing.

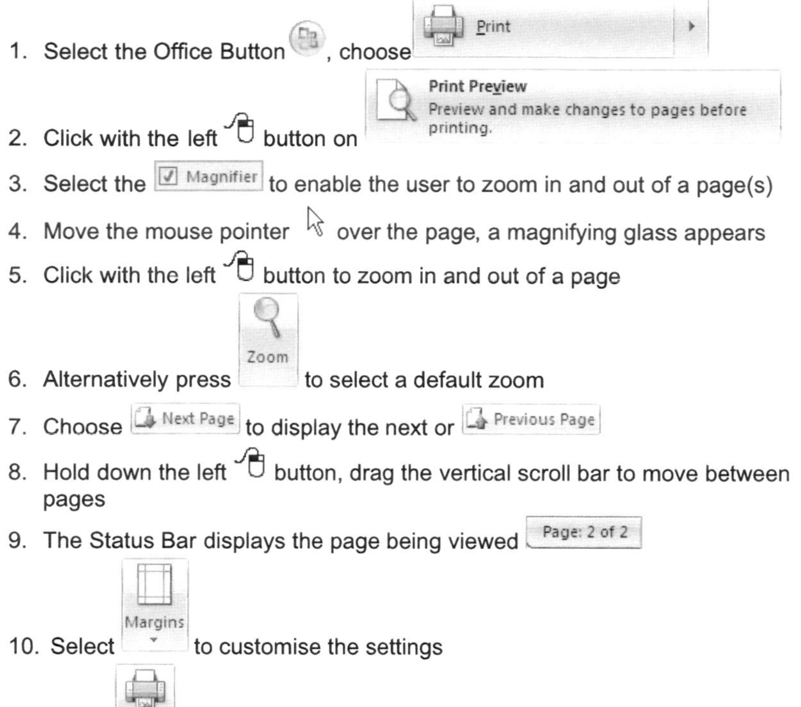

1. Select the Office Button, choose Print
2. Click with the left button on Print Preview (Preview and make changes to pages before printing.)
3. Select the Magnifier to enable the user to zoom in and out of a page(s)
4. Move the mouse pointer over the page, a magnifying glass appears
5. Click with the left button to zoom in and out of a page
6. Alternatively press Zoom to select a default zoom
7. Choose Next Page to display the next or Previous Page
8. Hold down the left button, drag the vertical scroll bar to move between pages
9. The Status Bar displays the page being viewed Page: 2 of 2
10. Select Margins to customise the settings
11. Select Print to open the Print dialog box

Printing a Document

1. Click on the Office Button, choose

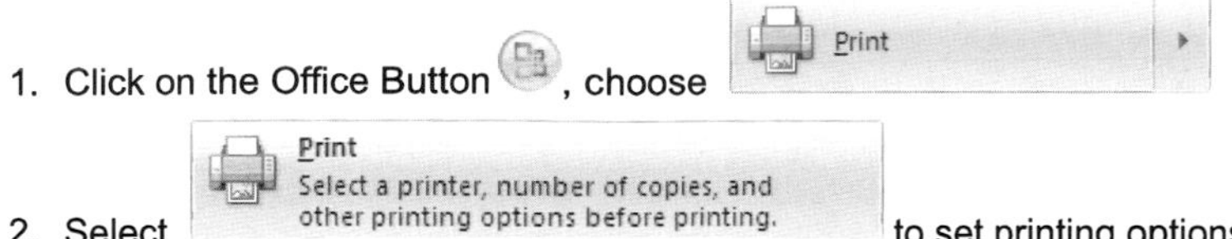

2. Select to set printing options
3. The Print dialog box appears

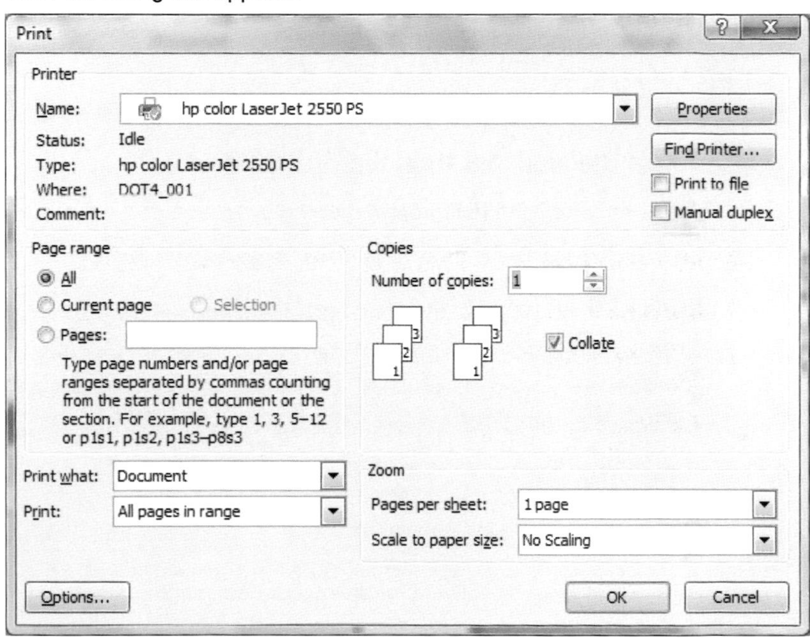

Figure 26

4. The **N**ame area highlights the printer to be used
5. In the Page range enter the selected page numbers to be printed
6. Alternatively select **A**ll, or Curr**e**nt page
7. Select the Number of **c**opies required
8. In the Print **w**hat box, click on the downward pointing arrow to view the options, choose Document
9. Click OK

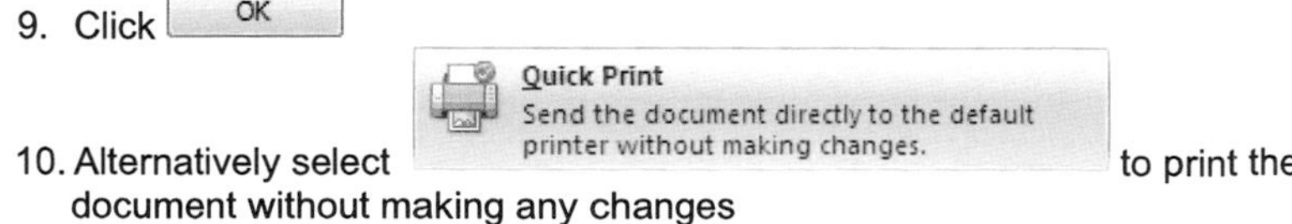

10. Alternatively select to print the document without making any changes

Bullets and Numbering

Bullets are a useful way in which to create a list of items in a document.

Creating a Bulleted List as you type

1. Click on the Bullets icon from the Paragraph Grouping
2. Type out the first item in your list
3. Press return or Enter, type out the next item
4. Press return or Enter
5. Click to deselect the bulleting

To Create a Bulleted List from the Bullet Library

1. Select from the Paragraph Grouping
2. Click on the downward arrow to bring up the Bullet Library

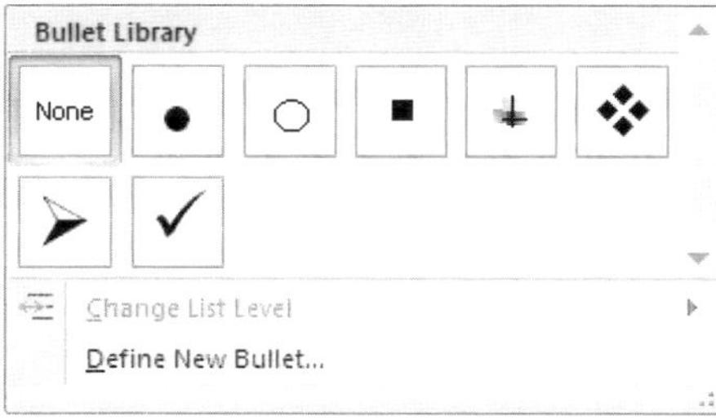

Figure 27

3. Click on the required bullet to return to your document
4. Type out the first item in your list
5. Press return or Enter, type out the next item
6. Press return or Enter
7. Click to deselect bulleting

To Create a Customised Bulleted List

1. Select the Bullets icon from the Paragraph Grouping
2. Click on the downward arrow to bring up the Bullet Library

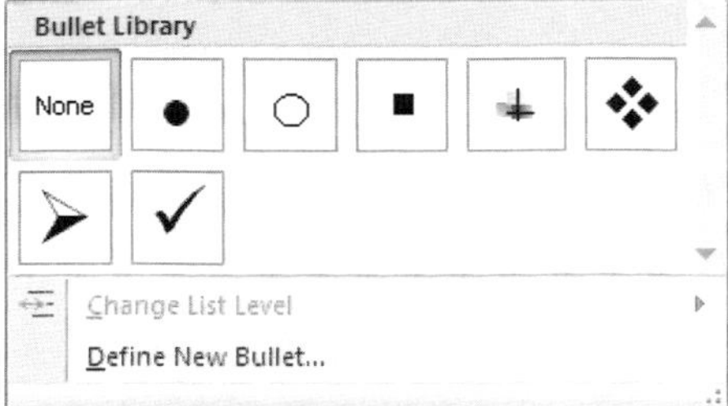

Figure 28

3. Select Define New Bullet...
4. The Define New Bullet dialog box appears

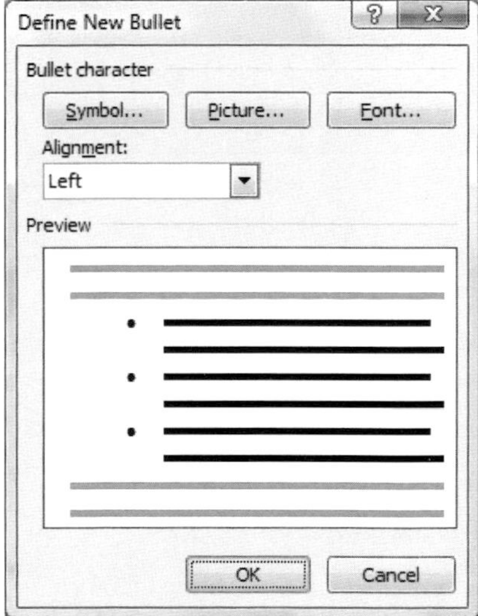

Figure 29

5. Select Font... to change the colour of the bullet
6. Click OK twice to return to the document
7. Type out your bulleted list, press Enter twice to turn off the bulleted style

Creating a Numbered List

1. Click on the Numbering icon from the Paragraph Grouping
2. Type out the first item in your list
3. Press return or Enter, type out the next item
4. Press return or Enter
5. Click to deselect the numbering

To Continue a Numbered List in a Document

1. Select the position where you want the numbered list to continue
2. Select click the downward arrow to select the Numbering Library
3. Select Set Numbering Value...
4. The Set Numbering Value dialog box appears

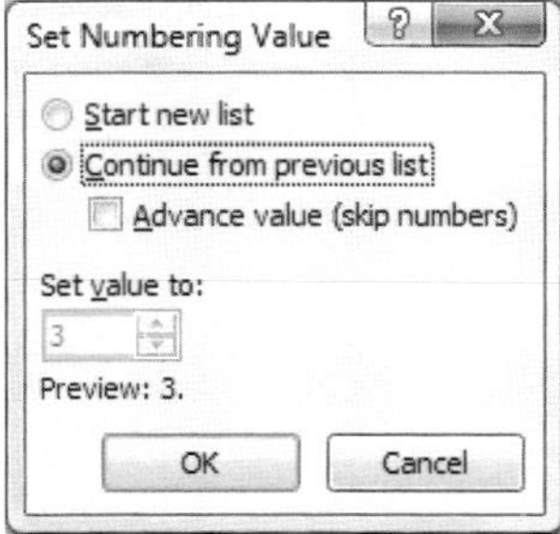

Figure 30

5. Choose Continue from previous list, click OK

To Restart Numbering

1. Select the position where you want the numbered list to continue
2. Select from the Paragraph Grouping
3. Click on the downward arrow to select the Numbering Library
4. Select Set Numbering Value...
5. The Set Numbering Value dialog box appears

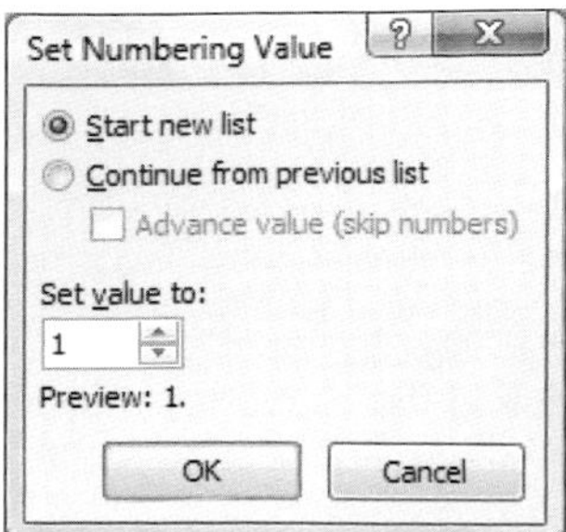

Figure 31

6. Click **S**tart new list, press OK

To create your own Numbering Style

Figure 32

1. Choose one of the above styles or a style of your choice
2. In a new document create the chosen list by typing out either

   a) Leeds or

   i) France or

   your own style
3. Press Enter to move down a line, continue typing the list
4. Press Enter twice to turn off the style

Exercise 4: - Bulleted Lists

New Zealand

New Zealand is known as a land of beauty, offering the visitor the excitement of its cosmopolitan cities to the tranquillity of its mountains and landscapes. Positioned amongst the Pacific to the east and the Tasman Sea to the west, New Zealand experiences warm moist climates, the volcanoes in the centre of the islands are occasionally active.

But it's not only the country that's beautiful, New Zealand has beautiful people. With a mixed population, one third of the people are Polynesian, the Maori culture of wood carving, weaving and music can be seen everywhere. The people are young more than half are less than 30 years old. Sheep and cattle ranching is the biggest business with three cattle and 20 sheep to every human.

Auckland with its cosmopolitan atmosphere has high-rise buildings towering over the city and is an important distribution centre. New Zealand is also one of the biggest exporters of seafood and the second biggest exporter of wool as well as exporting Kiwi fruits, oranges and lemons. New Zealand exports more dairy products and lamb than any other nation.

1. Type the text shown above
2. Centre and Underline the heading
3. Change the heading Font to Times New Roman with a Font size of 18
4. Ensure the words New Zealand throughout the text have hard spaces
5. Create a bulleted list at the end of the document of items exported by New Zealand
6. Spell check the document
7. Create a centred Header stating the name of your organisation
8. Create a Footer with your name on the left and today's date on the right
9. Use Print Preview to view the document
10. Save and close the document

Introducing Simple Tables

Two quick ways to create a table within a document is by using the Table Grouping commands or by using the Insert Table feature.

Creating a Table using the Table Grouping Commands

1. Open a new document
2. Click the left button in the document where the table needs to appear
3. Select Insert, choose Table from the Tables Grouping
4. The Insert Table menu appears

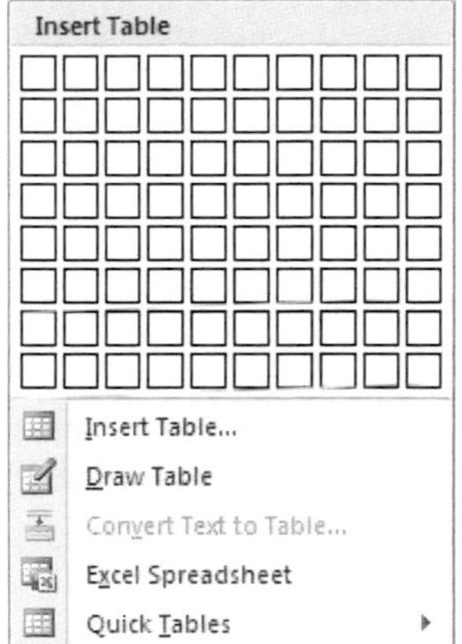

Figure 33

5. Using the mouse highlight the number of columns and rows required

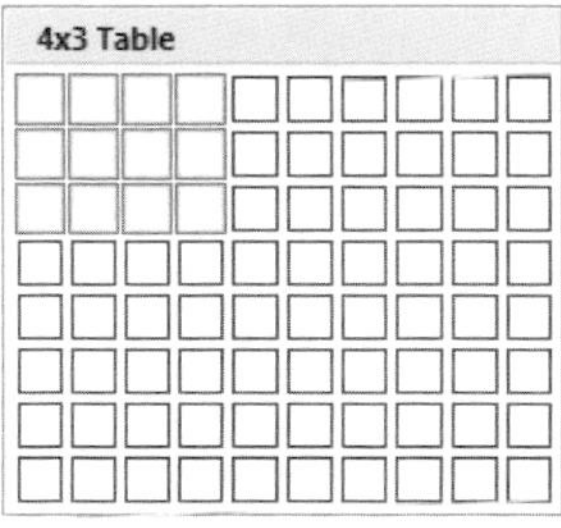

Figure 34

6. Let go of the mouse to install the table in the document

¤	¤	¤	¤
¤	¤	¤	¤
¤	¤	¤	¤

¶

Figure 35

7. Press the Tab key to move from cell to cell within the table
8. To move back a cell press the Shift and Tab keys
9. Alternatively move using the keys on the keyboard ↑ ↓ ← →
10. Press the Tab key to insert a row when you reach the end of the table

Inserting Rows

1. Click with the right button in a cell where a row is to be inserted
2. Select Insert to open the menu box

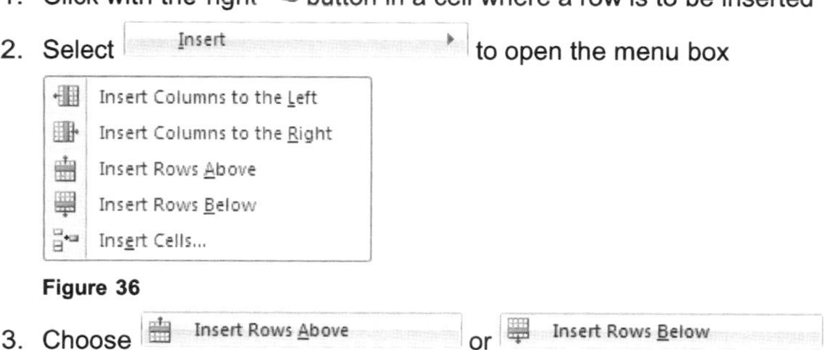

Figure 36

3. Choose Insert Rows Above or Insert Rows Below
4. A new row is inserted

Inserting Columns

1. Click with the right button in a cell where a column is to be inserted
2. Select Insert to open the menu box

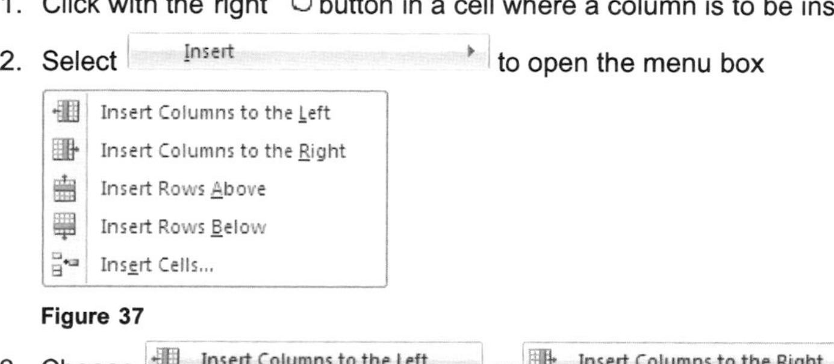

Figure 37

3. Choose Insert Columns to the Left or Insert Columns to the Right
4. A new column is inserted

To Merge or Join Cells in a Table

1. Click with the right button in the first cell of the table
2. Hold the Shift key down, click in the last cell that you want to merge
3. Click with the right button, select Merge Cells
4. The selected cells are merged into one cell

To Delete Rows in a Table

1. Click in the row to be deleted
2. Press the right button, select Delete Cells...
3. The Delete Cells dialog box appears

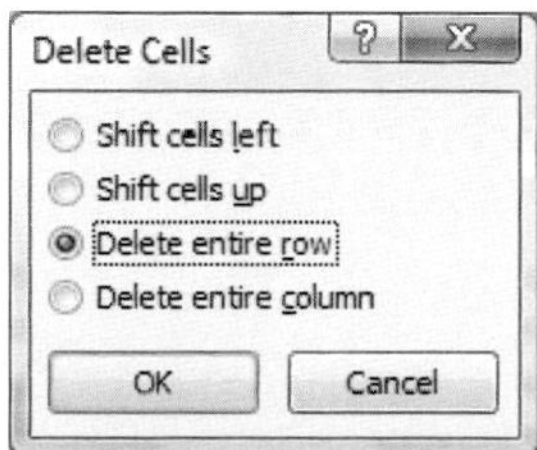

Figure 38

4. Select Delete entire row, press OK

To Delete Columns in a Table

1. Click in the column to be deleted
2. With the right button select Delete Cells...
3. The Delete Cells dialog box appears

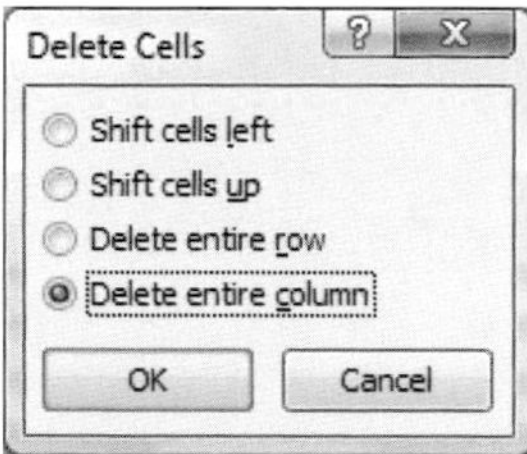

Figure 39

4. Select Delete entire column, press OK

Creating a Table using the Insert Table Feature

1. Click in the document where the table is to appear
2. Select Insert, choose Table from the Tables Grouping
3. The Insert Table menu appears

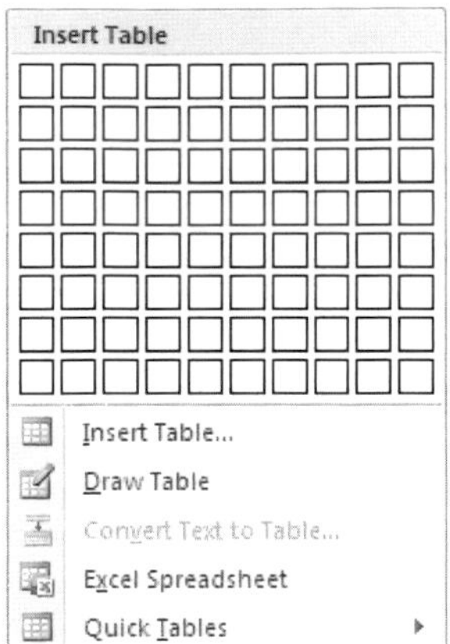

Figure 40

4. Select Insert Table... with the left button
5. The Insert Table dialog box appears

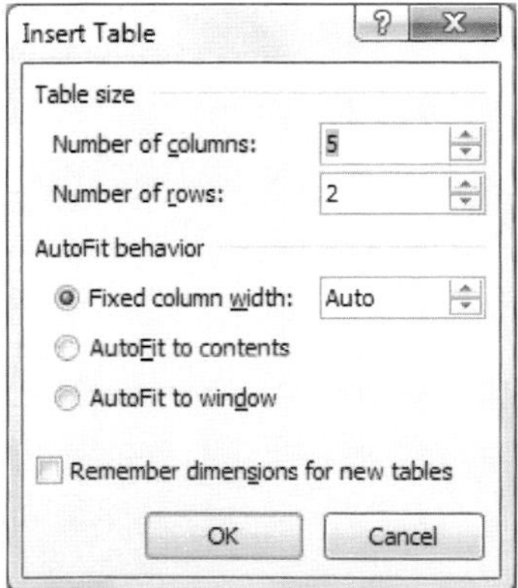

Figure 41

6. Enter the Number of **c**olumns and **r**ows for the required table
7. Select Fixed column **w**idth, choose Auto
8. Press OK

9. Select a style from the Table Styles Grouping
10. Extend the menu by clicking on the downward arrow

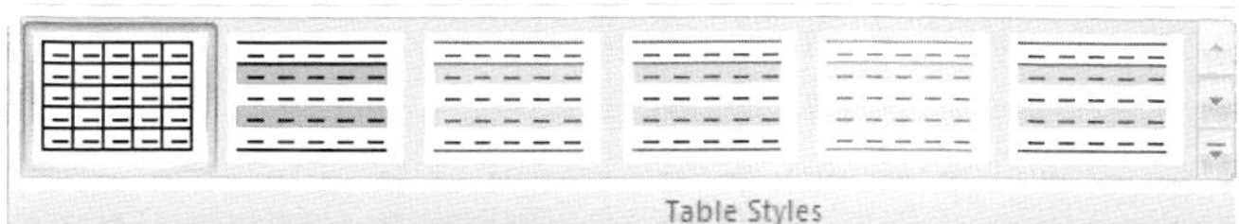

Figure 42

11. The selected style appears in your document

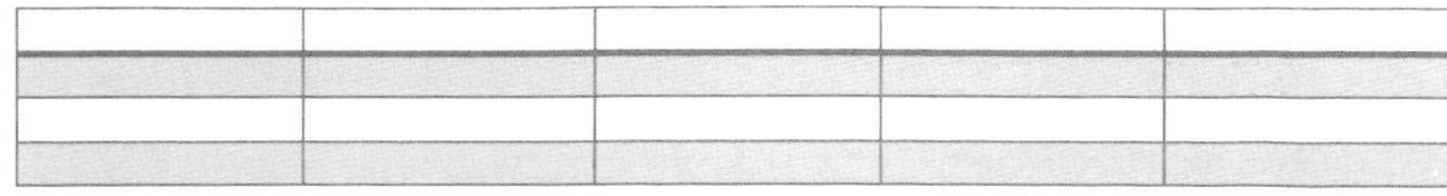

Figure 43

Exercise 5: - Creating a Simple Table

Product	**Price £**
Garden Peas	0.85
Coke	1.27
Lettuce	0.69
Tomatoes	0.99
Potatoes	0.62
Yoghurt	0.37
Cherries	1.23
Lamb Chops	5.00
Bananas	1.10
Corn Flakes	1.65
Total	**£13.77**

1. Produce the above table using any format
2. Insert a row between Garden Peas and Coke and add Apples at 0.59
3. Delete Corn Flakes from the list
4. Insert a new column to the right of the table
5. Name the column “Use By Date”
6. Find three fruits and replace them with ones of your choice
7. Choose a different style and update the table
8. Insert a Row at the beginning of the table, merge the cells
9. Name the row “Shopping List”, highlight and centre the text
10. Save the document

Section 2: Intermediate Level Objectives

- Working with Tables
- Section and Page Breaks
- Setting Tabs
- Working with Styles
- Creating New Styles
- Define and Locate Bookmarks
- Generate a Table of Contents
- Creating an Index
- The AutoSummarise Feature
- Reviewing a Document using Track Changes
- Using Comments
- Creating a Mail Merge
- Using Mail Merge to Create Labels
- Templates

Note: If you are working in Windows XP instead of Windows Vista, dialog boxes may look different but function in a similar way.

Working with Tables

Using the AutoFit Feature

The AutoFit Feature automatically resizes rows and columns to the size of their contents.

1. Click anywhere inside the table
2. Select Layout from the Table Tools Grouping
3. Choose AutoFit to expand the menu

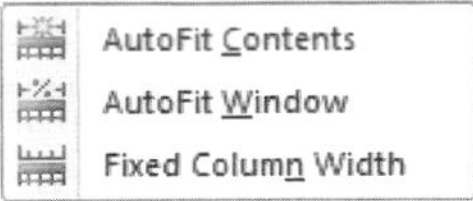

Figure 44

4. Choose AutoFit Contents to automatically adjust the cells to fit their contents

The AutoFormat Feature

The AutoFormat Feature allows the user to quickly customise a table to suit individual needs.

1. Select the table requiring formatting
2. Choose Design from the Table Tools Grouping
3. Choose the Table Styles Command

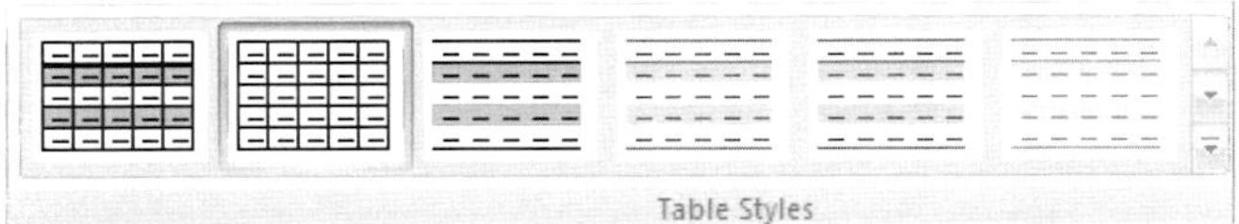

Figure 45

4. Click on the downward pointing arrow to expand the menu

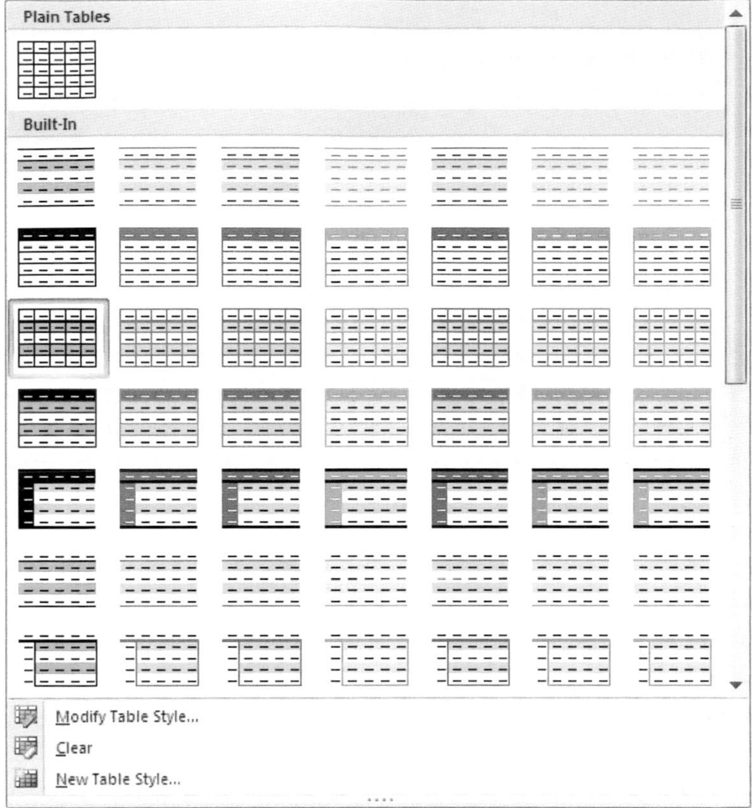

Figure 46

5. Select a style of your choice
6. Choose Modify Table Style...
7. The Modify Style dialog appears

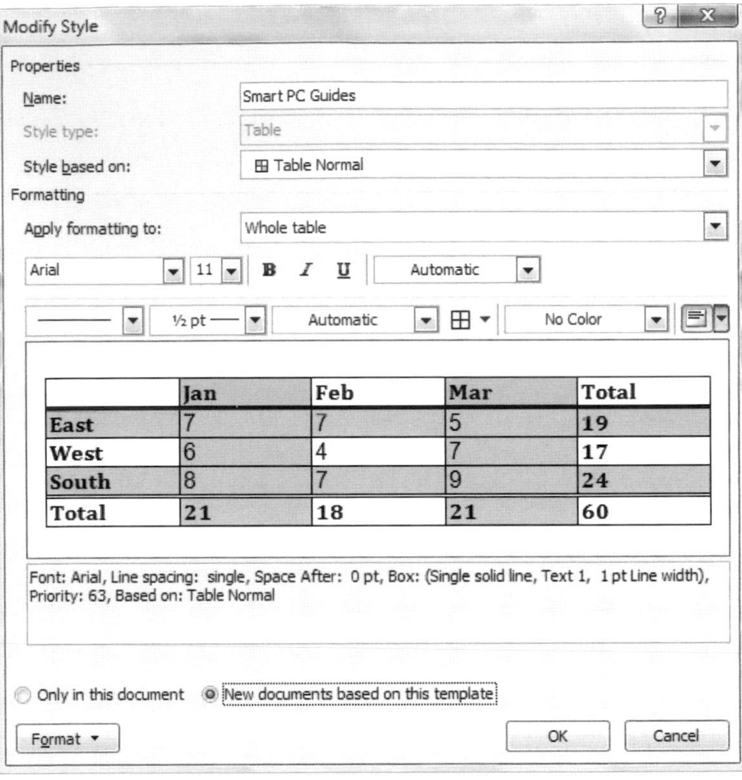

Figure 47

8. Choose Name and type Smart PC Guides

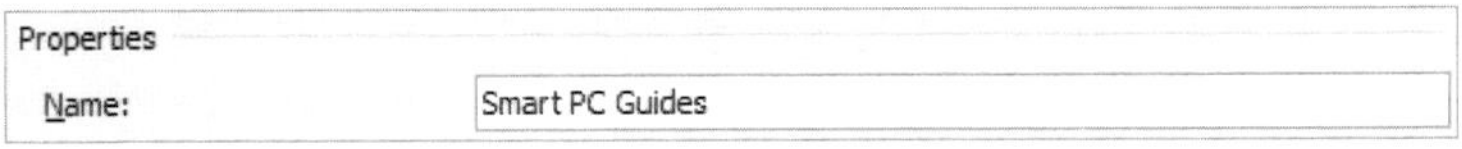

Properties
Name: Smart PC Guides

Figure 48

9. Change the Font style to Arial and format the table as required
10. Select the option Only in this document or New documents based on this template

Only in this document   New documents based on this template

Figure 49

11. Press OK

To Delete a Table Style

1. Choose Design
2. Click on the downward pointing arrow to expand the Table Styles menu
3. Move the mouse pointer over Custom, Smart PC Guides appears

Figure 50

4. Click with the right button, select Delete Table Style
5. The following prompt appears

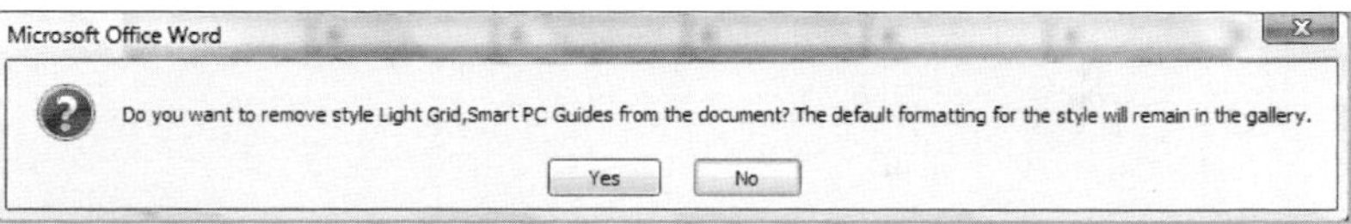

Figure 51

6. Press Yes

Creating a Table using the Drawing Pencil

1. Select a table, choose Insert
2. Click with the left button on the downward arrow of the Table command

Figure 52

3. Select Draw Table
4. The drawing pencil appears
5. In the status bar the following prompt appears

Click and drag to create table and to draw rows, columns and borders.

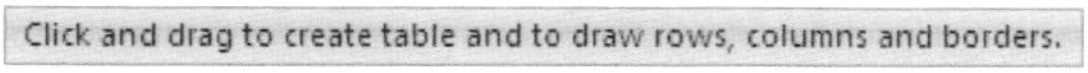

Figure 53

6. Drag using the left button to create a table by drawing rows and columns
7. The Table Tools Group appears as the table is being created
8. To format, change line colour, or use the Eraser, select the appropriate command from the Draw Borders Grouping

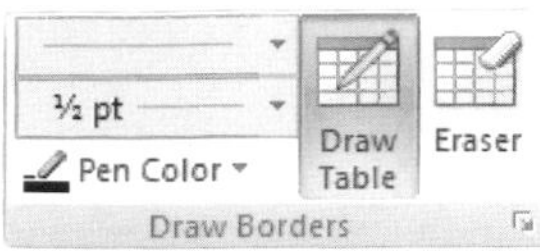

Figure 54

9. Alternatively use Alt N T D to display the drawing pencil

Rotating Text in a Table

To change text direction within selected cells

1. Select the text in the table to be rotated, choose Layout, Text Direction
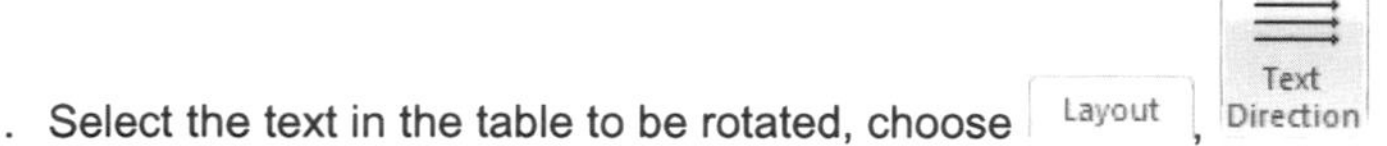
2. To merge cells, highlight the cells in the table to be merged together
3. Select Merge Cells
4. To split cells, click in the cell to be split into smaller rows or columns
5. Choose Split Cells, the Split Cells dialog box appears

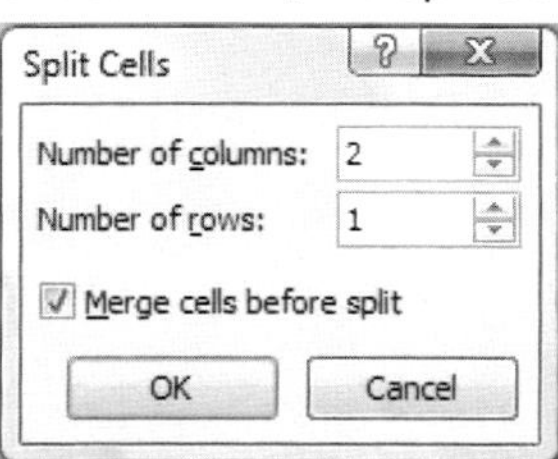

Figure 55

6. Enter the number of columns or rows, click OK
7. To delete lines from the table, select Design, choose

8. Click and drag with the left button on the line to be deleted
9. Release the left button
10. To switch off the Eraser click with the left button on

11. To sort items alphabetically or numerically select 

,

12. The Sort dialog box appears, select the required format, press OK

Exercise 6: - Creating a Booking Form

Smart PC Guides Travel Services		
Departure Information		
Reservation Reference:		Destination
UK Departure Airport		Name of Airport
Date of Travel		
Number of Nights		

Title	Initial	Surname (in Capitals)		Insurance		
				Yes	Delete YES if you have arranged alternative insurance which is valid for your travel dates	
				Yes		
				Yes		
				Yes		
				Yes		
				Yes		NAME OF INSURER:
				Yes		
				Yes		
				Yes		
				Yes		

Arrival Date	Hotel Name	Resort	No of Nights

Full Address and Telephone Number of First Named Adult			
		Telephone Number	
Signed		Date	

1. Create the above Booking Form using Tables
2. Save the form as Smart PC Guides Travel Services Booking Form

Different Types of Breaks

Page Breaks can be used to mark the point at which one page ends and the next page begins, whilst Section Breaks start a new section on the next page. Both are visible in Print Layout View, Outline and Draft View.

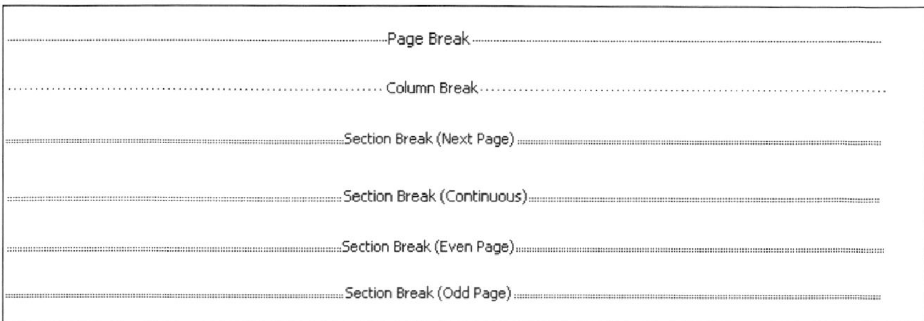

Figure 56

To Create a Section Break

1. Click Print Layout View
2. Select the place in a document where a section break is required
3. Select Page Layout, Breaks to extend the menu
4. Choose **Next Page** Insert a section break and start the new section on the next page.
5. Alternatively select Alt I B to display the Break dialog box

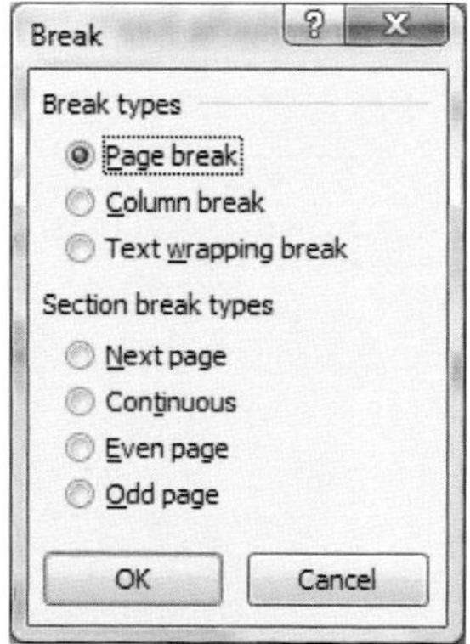

Figure 57

6. Select **N**ext page, press OK

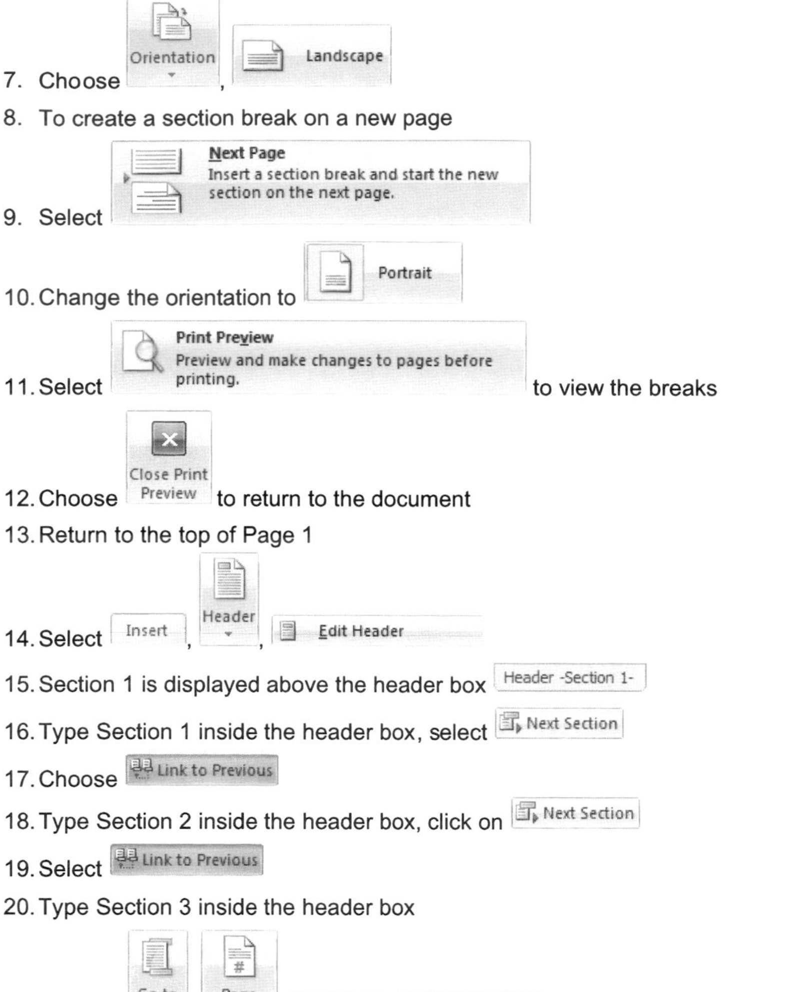

7. Choose Orientation, Landscape
8. To create a section break on a new page
9. Select Next Page
10. Change the orientation to Portrait
11. Select Print Preview to view the breaks
12. Choose Close Print Preview to return to the document
13. Return to the top of Page 1
14. Select Insert, Header, Edit Header
15. Section 1 is displayed above the header box
16. Type Section 1 inside the header box, select Next Section
17. Choose Link to Previous
18. Type Section 2 inside the header box, click on Next Section
19. Select Link to Previous
20. Type Section 3 inside the header box
21. Click on Go to Footer, Page Number, Bottom of Page, the gallery is displayed

22. Using the downward arrows on the scrollbar select Page X of Y

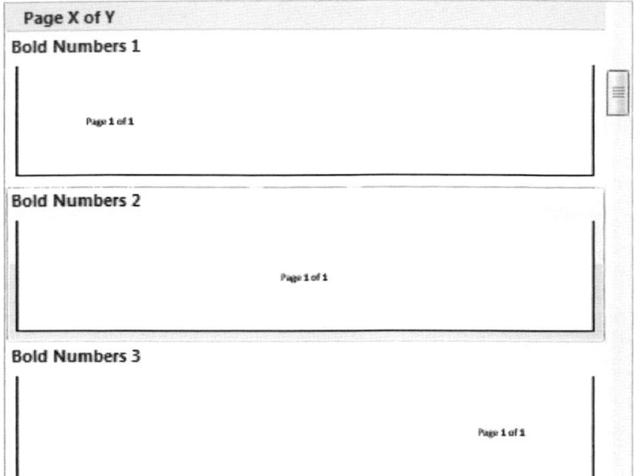

Figure 58

23. Choose the required option, page numbers appear at the foot of each page
24. Save the document as Working with Sections, preview the results

To Delete a Page, Column or Section Break

1. Select View, Draft, click the left button on the break you want to delete
2. Press the delete key to remove the break from the document
3. Alternatively press Alt W E to display the Draft View

Moving between Sections of a Document

1. Select 

2. Choose Next Section to display the next section
3. Click Previous Section to go back to the previous section
4. Select 

to switch from the header to the footer icon
5. Click 

to return to the Header
6. Press 

to return to the document
7. Alternatively select Print Layout View
8. Double click with the left button in the header or footer area
9. The Header & Footer Tools are displayed

Exercise 7: - Creating a Header and Footer

1. Open Smart PC Guides Travel Services Booking Form
2. Select a style from the gallery
3. Centre align and type Smart PC Guides Booking Form in the Header
4. Go to the Footer and insert Page 1 of 1 from the gallery
5. Save the document

Identify the Tab Stop Marker

Setting tabs allows you to quickly create and align information in a document.

1. To display the ruler in Print Layout or Web Layout select View
2. Click with the left button on Ruler
3. Alternatively select Alt W R

The default tab marker is set at 1.27cm

Figure 59

4. Select a new blank document
5. Click on the Show/Hide icon ¶ with the left button
6. Press Tab to move to the next default tab marker below the ruler
7. A tab stop is identified by a vertical grey line
8. The default tab is left aligned meaning the text appears from the left

Different Tab and Indent Icons

The following tab icons are displayed on the left hand side of the ruler.

Icons	Description of Icons in the Ruler
	Left Tab
	Centre Tab
	Right Align Tab
	Decimal Tab
	Bar Tab
	First Line Indent
	Hanging Indent

Figure 60

Setting Tabs from the Ruler

1. Move the mouse pointer over the left align icon
2. Click with the left button, the icon changes with each click displaying the different tab options
3. Choose the left alignment tab
4. Move the mouse pointer to 3cm on the ruler

5. Click with the left button, the left tab is set
6. Set a right tab at 13cm and a decimal tab at 7.5cm
7. Insert a bar tab at 5cm and 10cm, the set tabs are shown below

Figure 61

Removing Tabs from the Ruler

1. Move the mouse pointer over the left align icon in the ruler
2. Click and hold down the left button
3. Drag the selected tab off the ruler, the tab is removed from the ruler

Setting Tabs using the Tabs Dialog Box

1. Select Home, click on the downward arrow from the Paragraph Grouping
2. The Paragraph dialog box appears

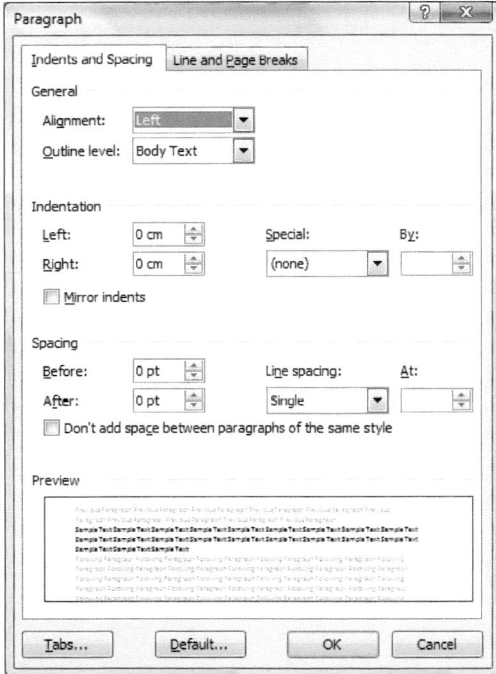

Figure 62

3. Select Tabs...

4. Alternatively press Alt O T
5. The Tabs dialog box appears

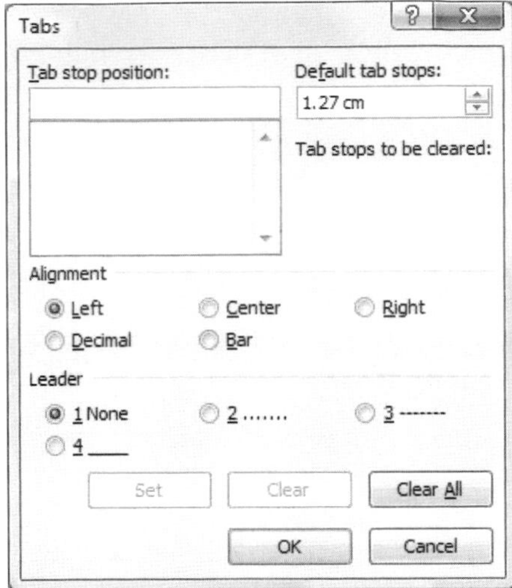

Figure 63

6. Select the Tab stop position
7. Type 3cm as the measurement for the tab stop
8. Select the Alignment Left, click Set
9. Repeat the above steps to set additional alignments
10. To remove an alignment click on the measurement
11. Click Clear, select OK
12. Selecting Clear All reverts back to the default tab
13. To modify a tab stop, double click with the left button on the tab marker
14. The Tabs dialog box is displayed

Exercise 8: - Creating Tabs using the Tabs Dialog Box

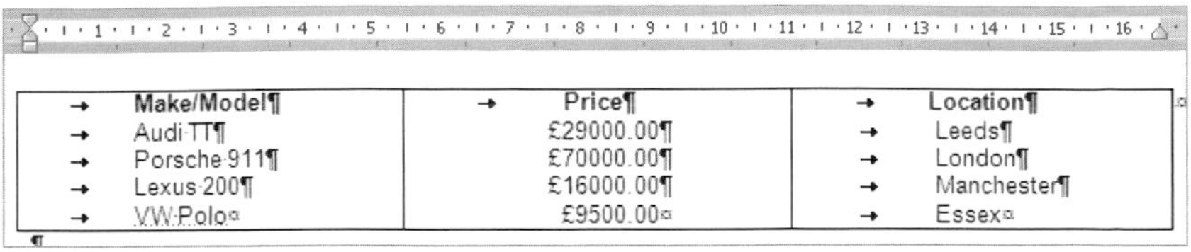

Make/Model	**Price**	**Location**
Audi TT	£29000.00	Leeds
Porsche 911	£70000.00	London
Lexus 200	£16000.00	Manchester
VW Polo	£9500.00	Essex

1. Select a new blank document
2. Create a table with 3 columns and 1 row
3. Set a centre tab in column 1 at 2.5cm
4. Use Tab to move to column 2, press F4
5. Use Tab to move to column 3, press F4
6. The centre tabs in column 2 and 3 are created
7. Type the above headings in each column, press Enter
8. Click the left button after the heading named **Make/Model**, press Enter
9. Create the new tab stops for the remaining text
10. Set a left tab in column 1 at 1.5cm
11. Set a decimal tab in column 2 at 3cm
12. Set a left tab in column 3 at 1.9cm
13. Type in the text as shown above
14. Save the document as Working with Tabs

What are Styles?

A style is a series of formats that can be applied to individual characters or entire paragraphs that enhance the appearance of documents. A table of contents can be created using the styles formatted in the document.

Styles enable you to change the format of documents, for example changing font, colour and typeface, alter alignments, indenting and line spacing, add number and bullet lists and create style headings and sub-headings. If styles are used in a document a Table of Contents can be generated automatically based upon the styles that have been formatted.

How to View Styles in a Document

1. Select Draft View or Outline View
2. Click the Office Button, select Word Options, Advanced
3. Using the downward arrow select Display
4. Alternatively select Alt F I A, scroll down to the Display area

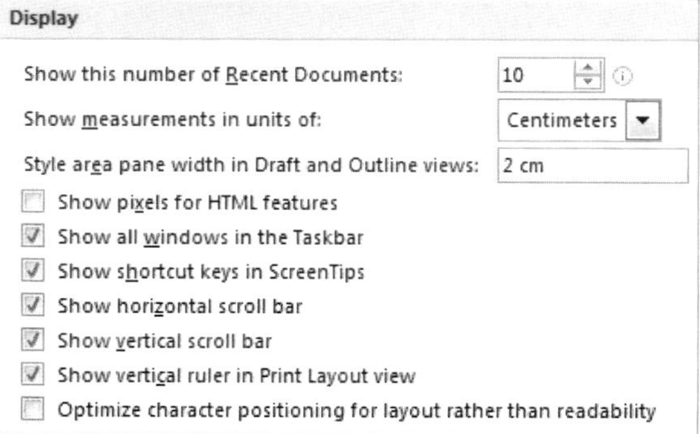

Figure 64

5. Change the measurement of the Style area pane width to 2cm
6. Select OK, the style area is displayed in the document

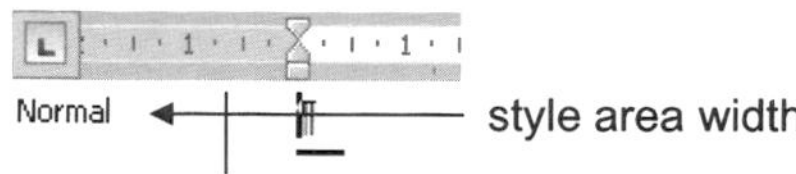

Figure 65

Working with Styles using the Formatting Toolbar

1. Select Home
2. Click on the downward arrow from the Styles Grouping

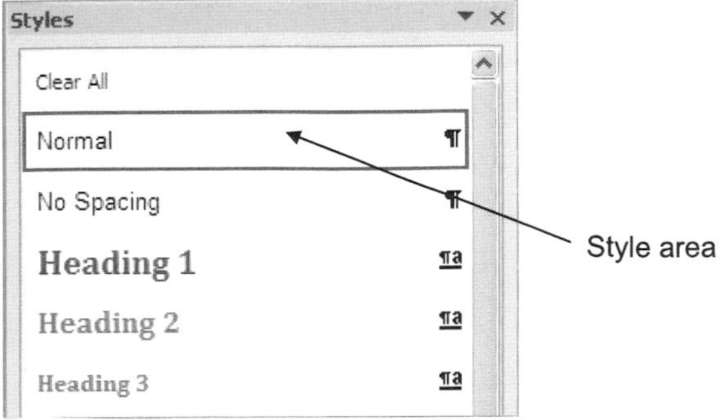

Figure 66

3. Select Heading 1, type Smart PC Guides
4. Select Heading 2, 3 and Normal Style to view the different styles
5. To clear formatting click on Clear All

To Modify a Style

1. Open a new blank document
2. Select Home
3. Click on the downward arrow from the Styles Grouping

Heading 1

Figure 67

4. Choose Heading 1, click with the right button on the downward arrow
5. Select Modify...
6. The Modify Style dialog box appears

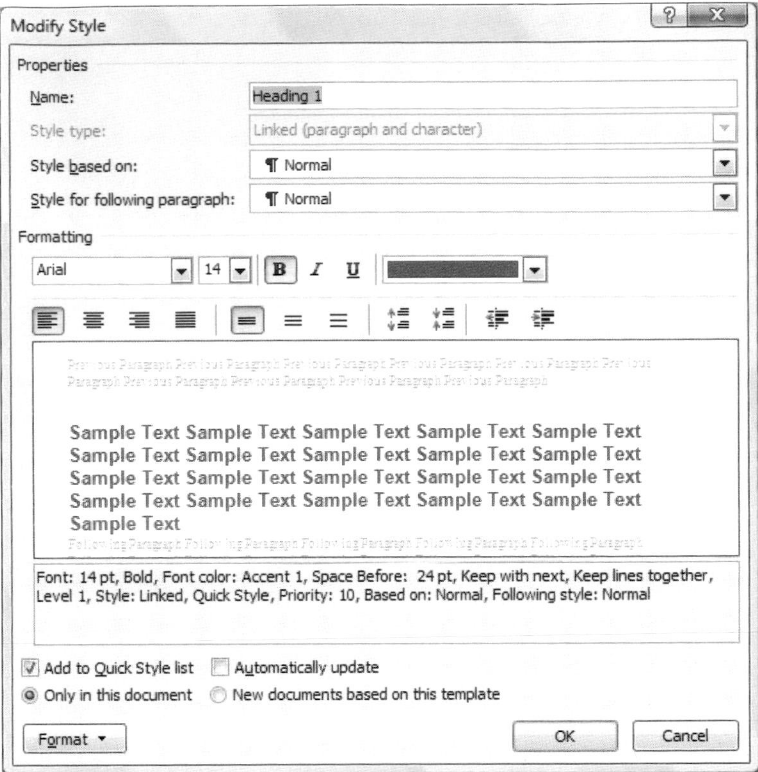

Figure 68

7. Change the formatting options as required, select Format

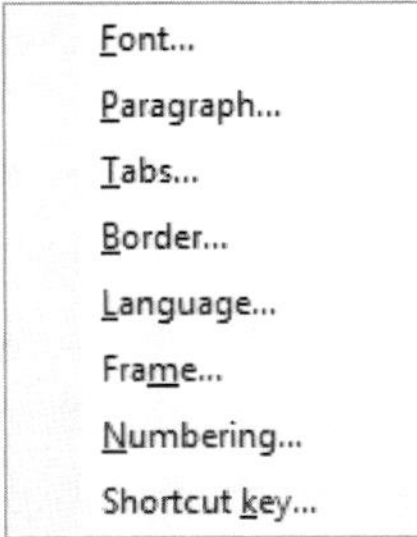

Figure 69

8. Click Font, change the colour, press OK twice
9. The modified style appears in the Styles task pane

Adding a Style to a Template

To add a style to a template, tick "New documents based on this template" in the Modify Style dialog box.

The Automatically Update Feature

Use the automatic update feature with extreme care. Any changes made to the alignment of a document using the "Automatically update" option changes all the text.

Creating a New Style

1. Click on a new blank document
2. Select Home, click on the downward arrow from the Styles Grouping
3. The Styles window is displayed
4. Choose Heading Style 1 from the Styles Gallery
5. Select the New Style icon
6. The Create New Style from Formatting dialog box appears

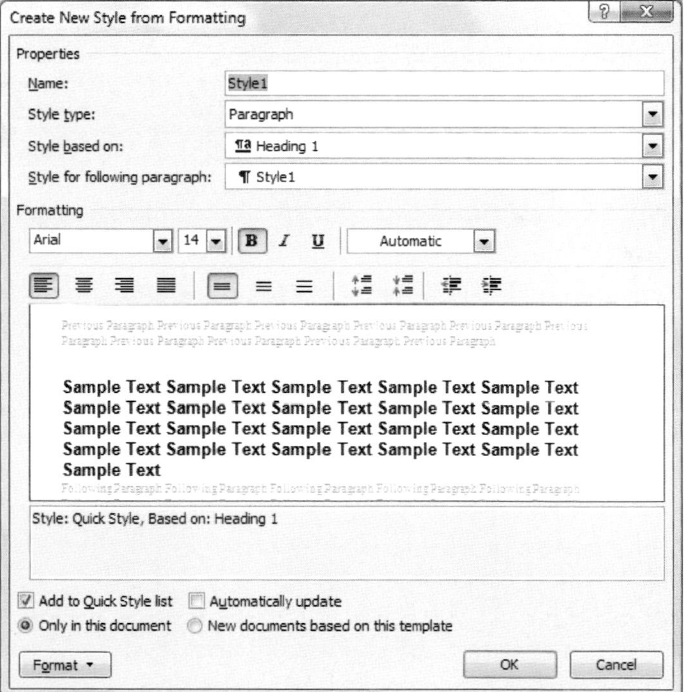

Figure 70

7. Select **N**ame, type Smart PC Guides New Style
8. Click Format ▾, modify the style to your requirements
9. Click OK, the Create New Style from Formatting dialog box appears
10. Select OK to return to the document
11. The style appears in the Styles area Smart PC Guides New Style

Assigning a Shortcut Key to a New Style

1. Choose Smart PC Guides New Style
2. Select Modify...
3. The Modify Style dialog box appears

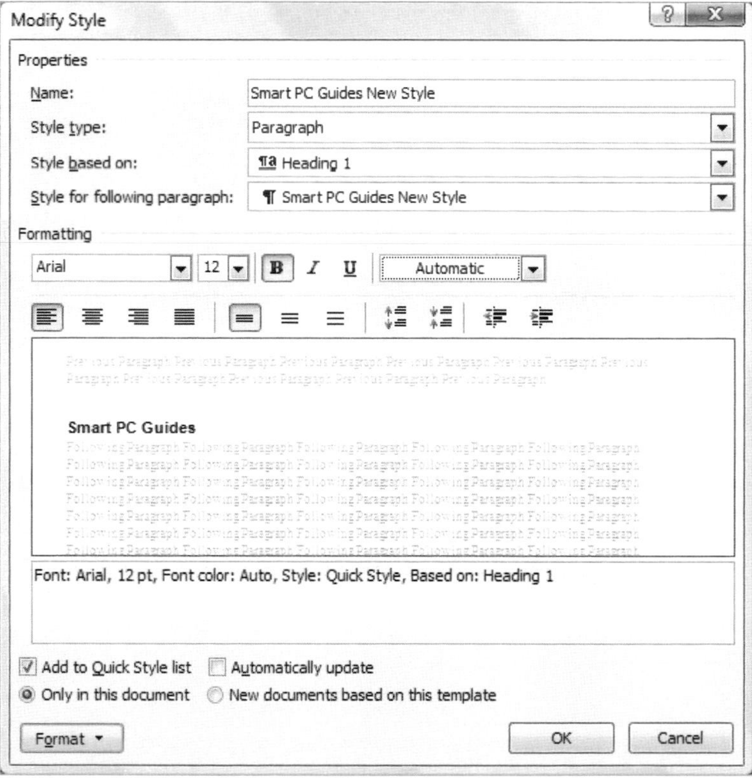

Figure 71

4. Click with the left mouse button on Format ▾
5. Select Shortcut key..., the Customise Keyboard dialog box appears

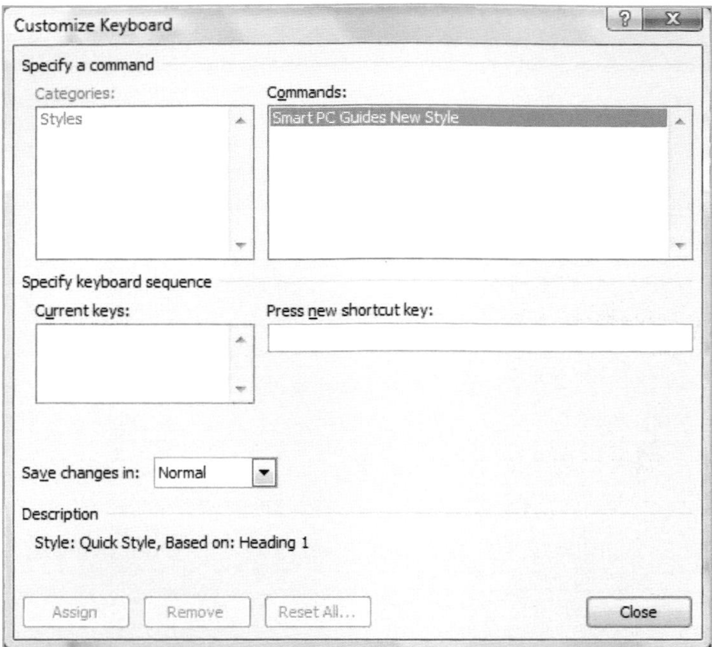

Figure 72

6. Smart PC Guides New Style appears in the Commands: box
7. Go to Press new shortcut key:
8. Hold down the Alt key, press 5
9. Click Assign, choose Close
10. Click with the left button in the New documents based on this template dialog box
11. Select OK

Deleting a Style already added to a Template

1. Select Home, click on the downward arrow from the Styles Grouping
2. Select Smart PC Guides New Style
3. Choose the Manage Styles icon, the Manage Styles dialog box appears

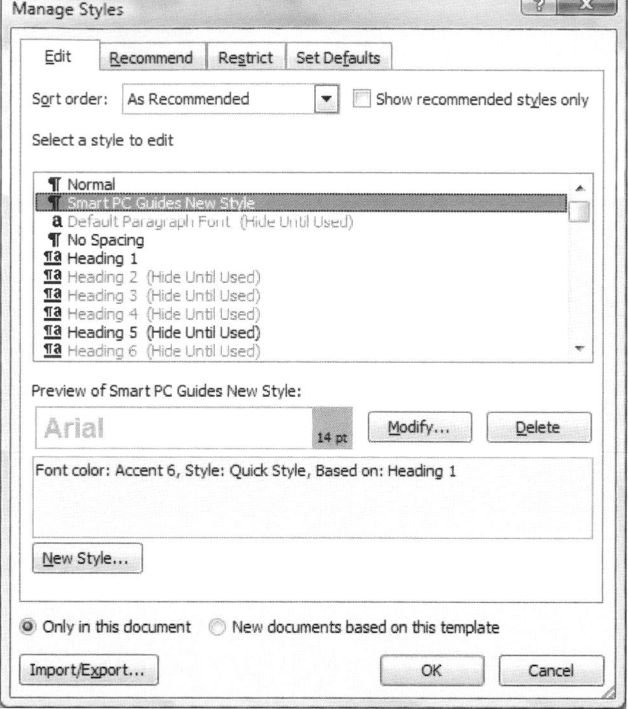

Figure 73

4. To delete the style from the template select Import/Export...
5. The Organiser dialog box appears

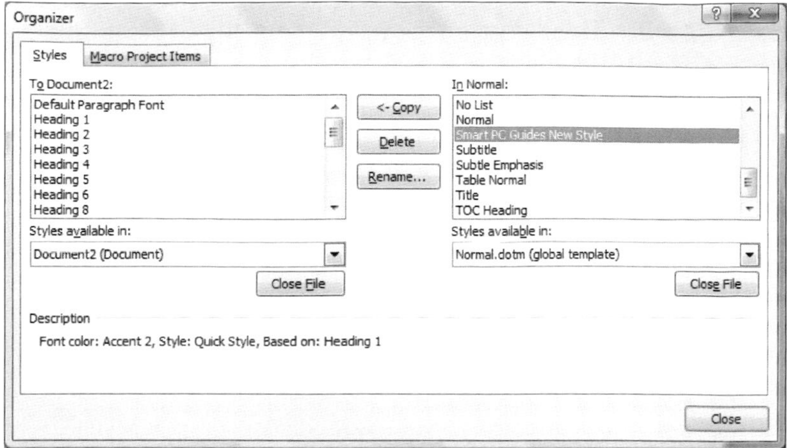

Figure 74

6. Go to **In** Normal area, select Smart PC Guides New Style
7. Press Delete

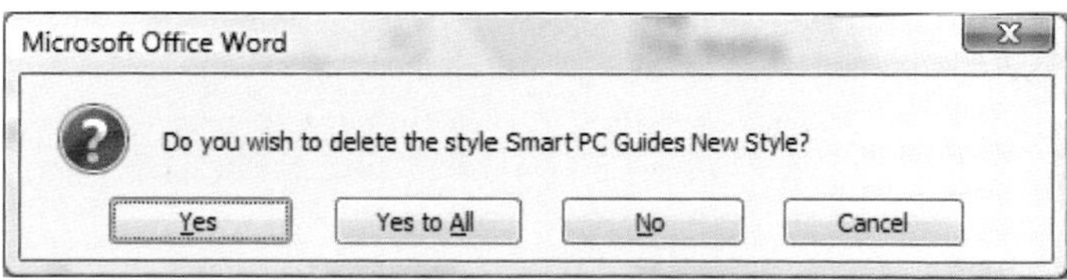

Figure 75

8. Press Yes to All to delete the style from the Normal.dotm (global template)
9. Click Close
10. Open a new document
11. Press Alt Ctrl Shift S to display the Styles window
12. Smart PC Guides New Style has been deleted

Exercise 9: - Creating a Document using Styles

1. Open a new blank document
2. On Page 1 select Heading Style 1, type Monday
3. Press Enter, select Heading Style 2, type Briefing at 10.00
4. On Page 2 select Heading Style 1, type Tuesday
5. Press Enter, select Heading Style 2, type Performance Review at 15.00
6. On Page 3 select Heading Style 1, type Wednesday
7. Press Enter, select Heading Style 3, type Progress Meeting 09.30
8. On Page 4 select Heading Style 1, type Thursday
9. Press Enter, select Heading Style 2, type Staff Appraisal at 14.15
10. On Page 5 select Heading Style 1, type Friday
11. Press Enter, select Heading Style 3, type Company Car New Criteria
12. Preview the document, check the newly created styles on each page
13. Save the document as Working with Styles
14. Close the document

Bookmarks

By setting a bookmark, text can be found easily for future reference.

To Add a Bookmark

1. Click with the left button in a document where you want to add a bookmark
2. Select Insert, Bookmark from the Links Grouping
3. Type the bookmark name

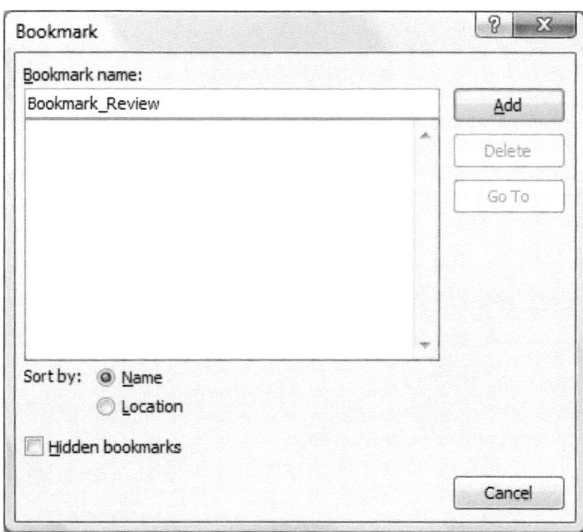

Figure 76

4. Click Add
5. Alternatively Alt N K displays the Bookmark dialog box

Note: The underscore character can be used to separate words when defining a name.

To Locate a Bookmark

1. Select Insert, Bookmark, select the bookmark name

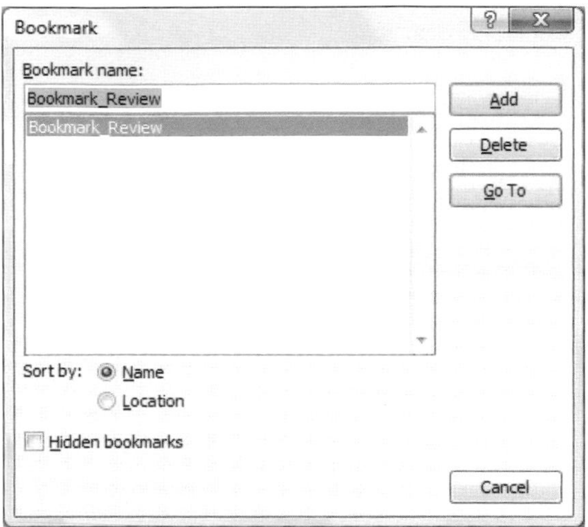

Figure 77

2. Click Go To, choose Close

3. Alternatively F5 displays the Go To dialog box

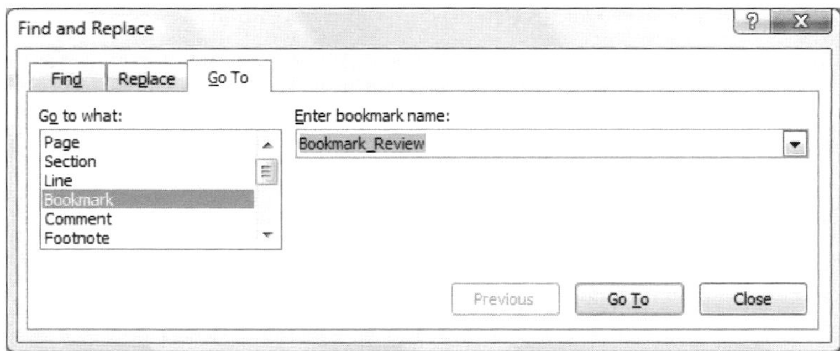

Figure 78

4. Click with the left button on the word Bookmark
5. Ensure the bookmark name **Bookmark_Review** is selected
6. Select Go To, click Close

To Delete a Bookmark

1. Select Insert, Bookmark, select the bookmark name
2. Click Delete, press Close

Creating a Table of Contents

A Table of Contents is a structured list of a document's content. If the document was constructed using styles, a Table of Contents can be generated automatically.

1. Open the document Working with Styles
2. Hold down the Ctrl and Home keys, go to page 1
3. Select Draft View and create a page break
4. Click in the new page, press Enter
5. Ensure the cursor is at the top of the new page
6. Choose Normal Style
7. Using the Formatting Grouping change the font to Arial, size 14, Bold

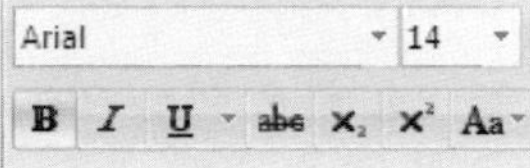

Figure 79

8. Centre align and type out Table of Contents on the first page
9. Press Enter, select, Align Left
10. Select References, Table of Contents, Insert Table of Contents...

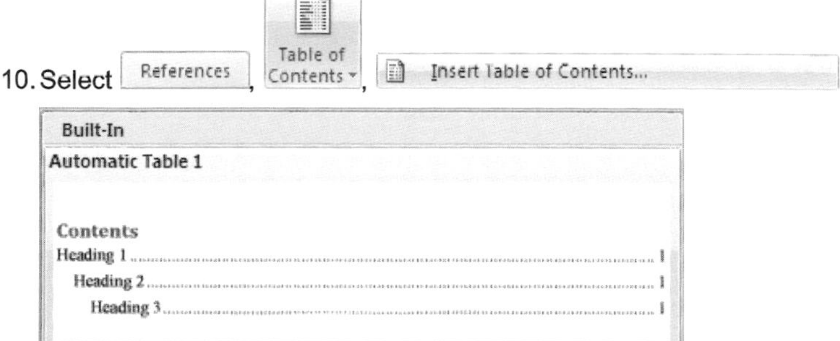

Figure 80

11. Alternatively Alt S T I displays the Table of Contents dialog box

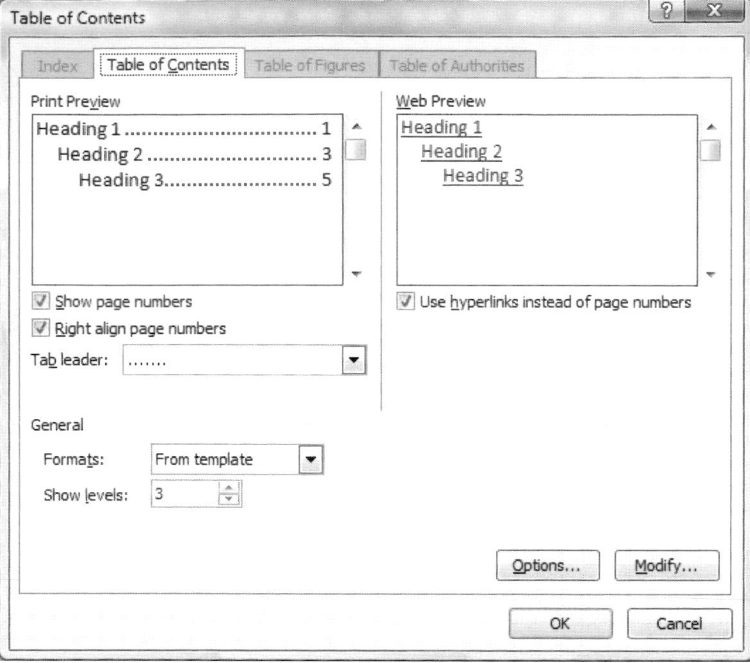

Figure 81

12. Print Pre**v**iew displays the layout of the Table of Contents
13. Select OK the Table of Contents appears in the document
14. Save the document

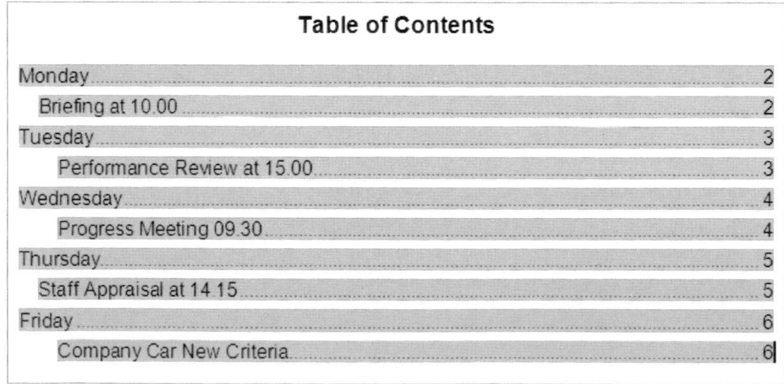

Figure 82

Exercise 10: - Updating a Table of Contents

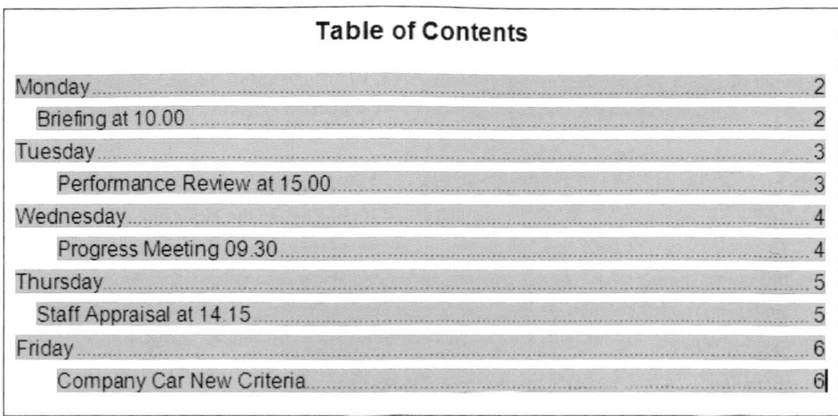

1. Open the document Working with Styles
2. Select View, Outline
3. Hold down Ctrl, move the mouse pointer over page 2
4. Click on the page number, the cursor appears on page 2
5. Change Briefing at 10:00 to Heading Style 3
6. Select References, click Update Table
7. Select Update entire table

8. Choose OK
9. Change Company Car New Criteria to Heading Style 2, click Update Table
10. Update the entire table, view the updated Table of Contents
11. Hold down Ctrl, move the mouse pointer over page 2
12. The mouse pointer changes to
13. Click on the page number, page 2 is displayed
14. Save the document

Indexes

Long documents normally have a reference guide at the back of the document known as an index. The index identifies keywords and subjects frequently used in a document.

Creating an Index

1. Open the document Working with Styles
2. Select References, Insert Index
3. The Index dialog box appears

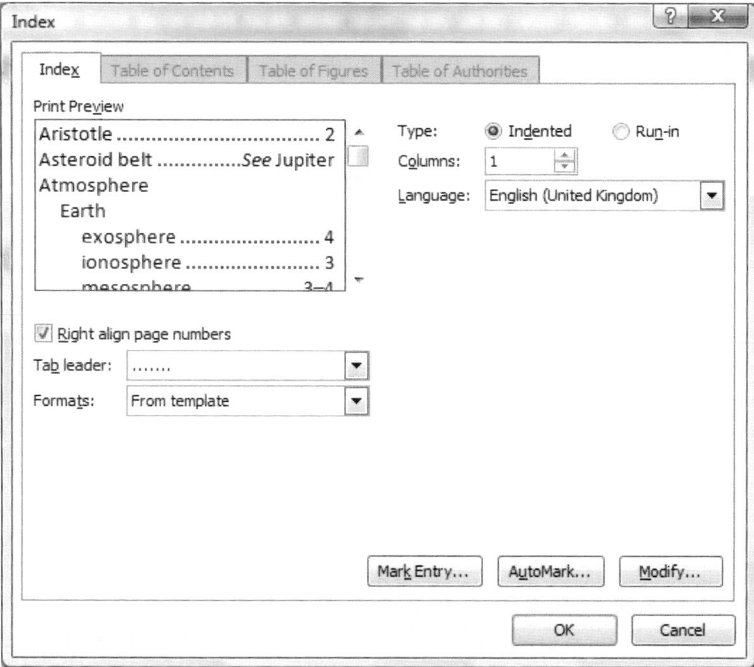

Figure 83

4. Select Type: Indented, choose Columns: 1
5. Change the dialog as below

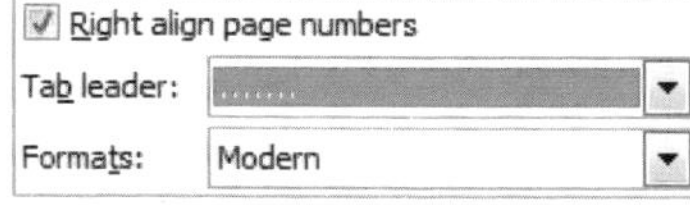

Figure 84

6. Click Mark Entry...

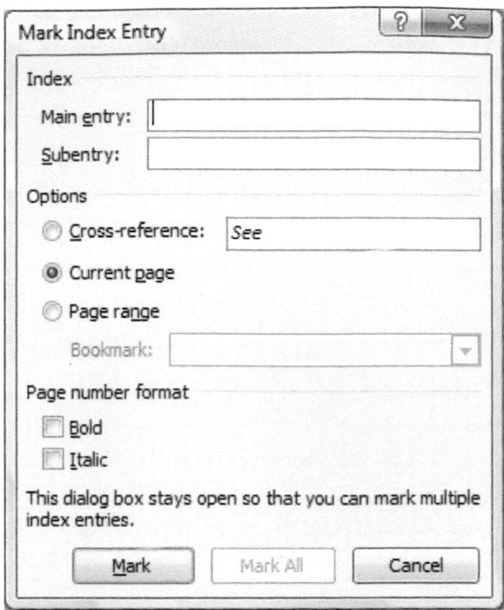

Figure 85

7. Create Main **e**ntries and **S**ubentries from the table below

Select	In Mark Index Type	Click
Main **e**ntry	Monday	Mark
Subentry	Briefing	
Main **e**ntry	Briefing	Mark
Subentry	Monday	
Main **e**ntry	Tuesday	Mark
Subentry	Performance	
Main **e**ntry	Performance	Mark
Subentry	Review	
Main **e**ntry	Review	Mark
Subentry	Tuesday	

Figure 86

8. Create Main **e**ntry and **S**ubentries for Wednesday to Friday, click Close
9. Go to the end of the document and create a new page
10. Select References, Insert Index, click Close

A

Appraisal
  Thursday.......5

B

Briefing
  Monday.......2

C

Company Car
  Friday.......6

F

Friday
  Company Car.......6

M

Monday
  Briefing.......2

P

Performance
  Review.......3
  Tuesday.......3
Progress
  Wednesday.......4

R

Review
  Performance.......3

T

Thursday
  Appraisal.......5
Tuesday
  Performance.......3

W

Wednesday
  Progress.......4

Figure 87

AutoSummarise

The AutoSummarise feature gives a score to each sentence based on the number of words most frequently used in a sentence. Word automatically summarises these key points to create a summary for others to read. The user can then select how much detail you wish to use in the summary.

To Read a Summary of an Online Document

1. Open or type the document that requires a summary
2. Click the Office Button, select Word Options, Customize
3. Select Commands Not in the Ribbon

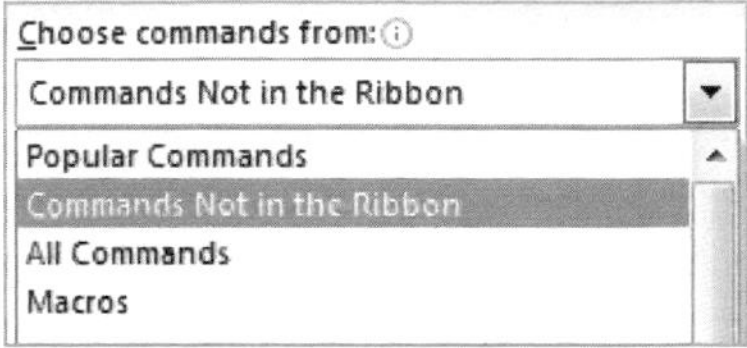

Figure 88

4. Scroll down using the downward arrow
5. Select AutoSummary Tools, click Add >>, OK
6. The AutoSummary icon appears on the quick access toolbar
7. Click on the downward arrow of the AutoSummary icon
8. Select Auto Summarize, the AutoSummarise dialog appears

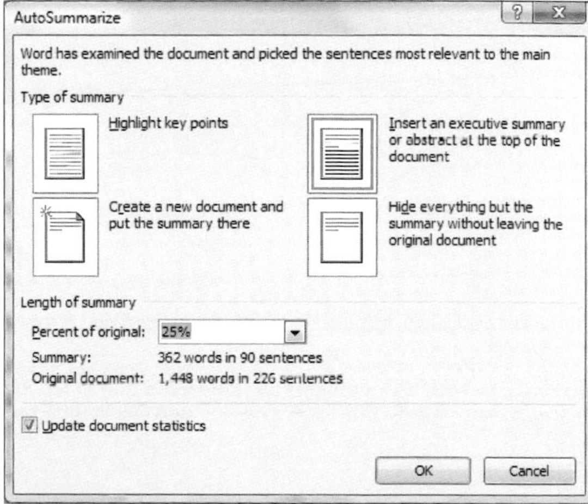

Figure 89

9. Select Type of summary
10. Click in the box to select the way you want to view the document
11. Select 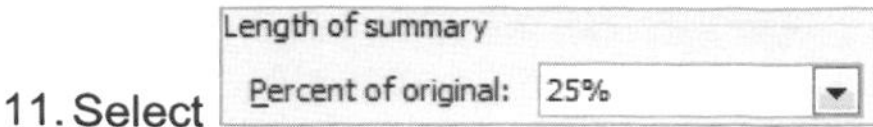

12. Use the arrow key to select how much detail is required
13. Click OK
14. The summary appears at the beginning of the document

To Alter the Display of a Document

1. Open or type the document that requires a summary
2. Click on the downward arrow of the AutoSummary icon
3. Select Auto Summarize
4. Select Type of summary

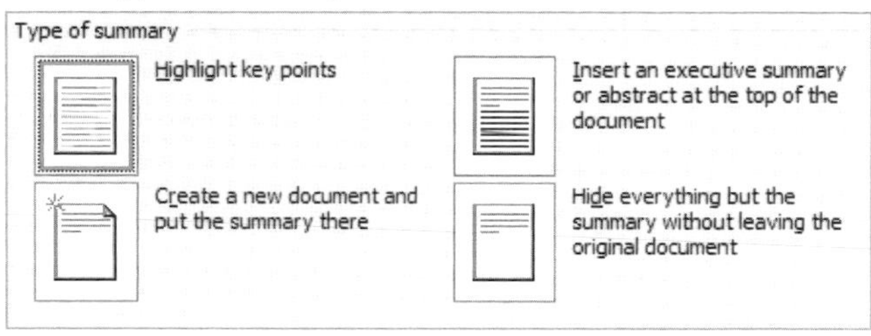

Figure 90

5. Click the <u>H</u>ighlight key points box, press OK

Display or Highlight Key Points in a Document

1. Open or type the document
2. Click on the downward arrow of the AutoSummary icon
3. Select Highlight/Show Only Summary
4. Press 

To Delete a Summary

1. To delete a summary, click the Undo icon on the quick access toolbar or modify the summary manually

Note: AutoSummarise automatically searches documents for keywords and sentences that represent discussed topics; it then copies these to Keywords and Comments boxes.

Reviewing a Document using Track Changes

Track Changes allows the user to make and view changes and comments made to a document.

How to use Track Changes

1. Open the document that requires changes to be made, select Review
2. Click on the downward arrow of the Track Changes icon Track Changes
3. Choose Track Changes
4. Highlight the text in the document that requires a change
5. Press Delete
6. The deleted text is displayed in the document ~~highlighted in red with a strikethrough~~
7. New text inserted is highlighted and underlined
8. Alternatively any changes made can be viewed in the margin
9. Select Balloons, click on the downward pointing arrow to expand the menu
10. Select

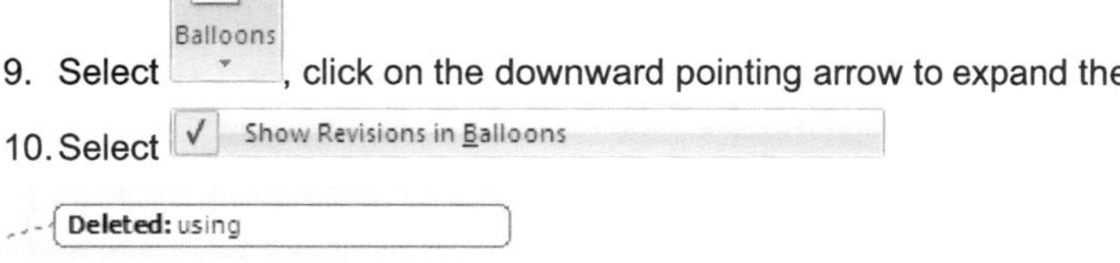

Figure 91

11. Click on Reviewing Pane in the Tracking Grouping
12. Select Reviewing Pane Vertical... to view changes made using the Reviewing Pane Vertically

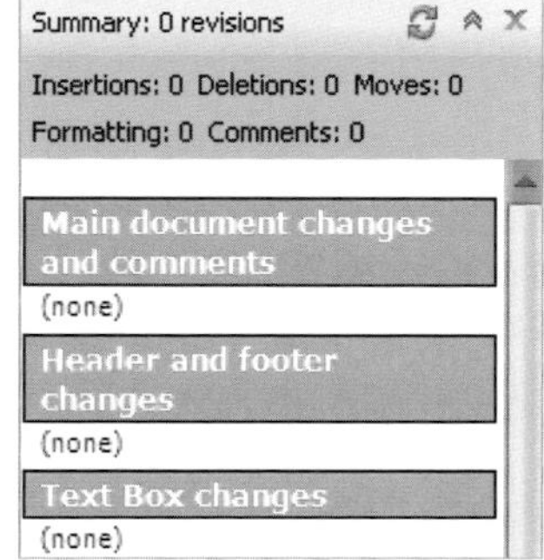

Figure 92

13. Or select Reviewing Pane Horizontal... to view changes made using the Reviewing Pane Horizontally

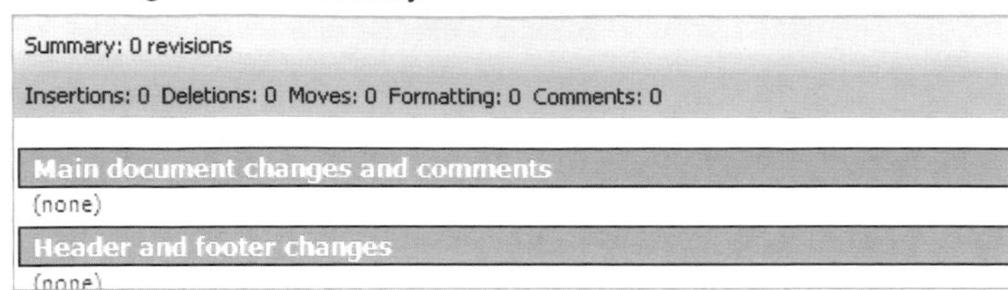

Figure 93

14. To choose how to see changes in the document
15. Select Final Showing Markup, click on the downward arrow to expand the menu

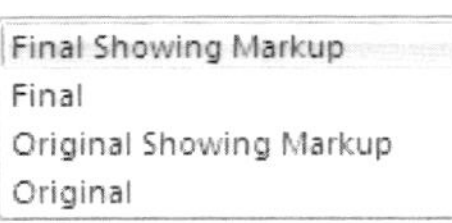

Figure 94

16. Select the required option

Using Comments

To Insert a Comment

1. Click where the comment is to appear in the document
2. Select Review, 

3. Type the required text in the balloon
4. The comment appears on the right-hand side of the document

Figure 95

To Edit a Comment

1. Select the comment to be edited
2. Click in the comment box on the right-hand side of the document
3. Edit the comment as required

To View Comments

1. Select the comment to be viewed
2. Choose Previous to see the previous comment in the document
3. Select Next to see the next comment in the document

To Delete a Comment

1. Select the comment to be deleted
2. Click in the balloon on the right hand side of the document
3. Select Delete
4. To delete all the comments in a document
5. Click on the downward arrow, choose Delete All Comments in Document

To Compare and Combine Multiple Copies of a Document

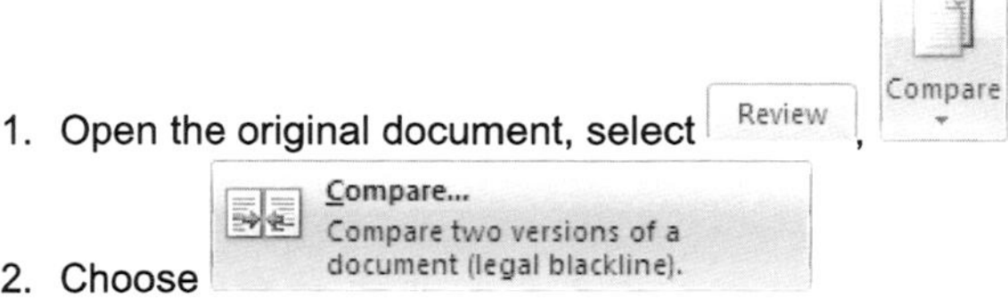

1. Open the original document, select Review, Compare
2. Choose Compare...
3. The Compare Documents dialog box appears

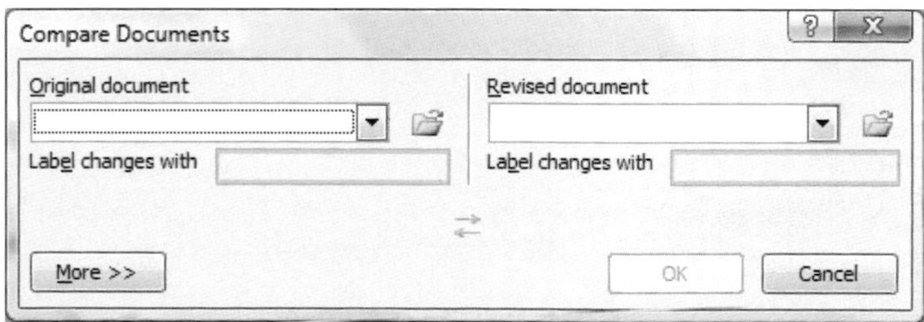

Figure 96

4. Click on the downward pointing arrow of the **O**riginal document box
5. Select and open the original document
6. Select and open the **R**evised document

Figure 97

7. The More >> icon in the Compare Documents dialog box enables the user to select the comparison settings and show changes to the documents
8. Select << Less to reduce the size of the Compare Documents dialog box
9. Choose OK

Note: Changes made in the More options automatically become the default options the next time the compare documents is used.

10. The documents appear on screen

Figure 98

11. To merge the documents
12. Select ,

13. The Combine Documents dialog box appears

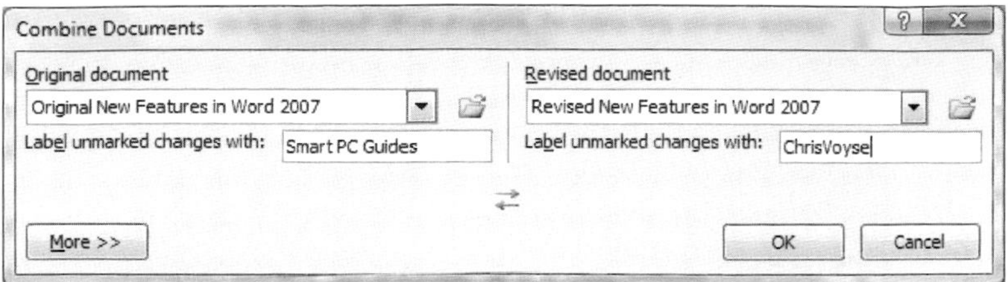

Figure 99

14. Select open the original document and the revised document

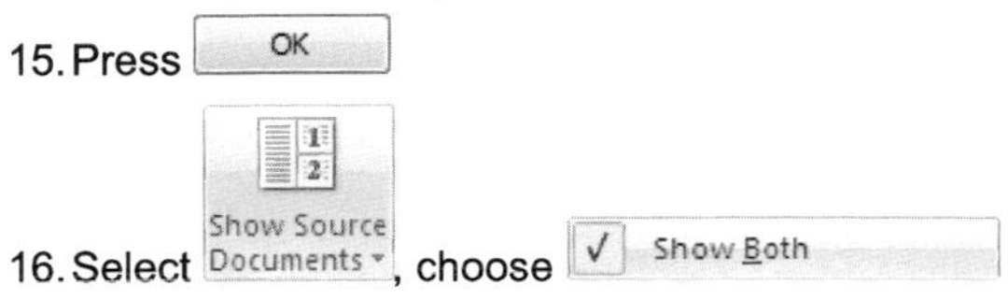

15. Press OK

16. Select Show Source Documents, choose Show Both

17. The combined document appears on screen

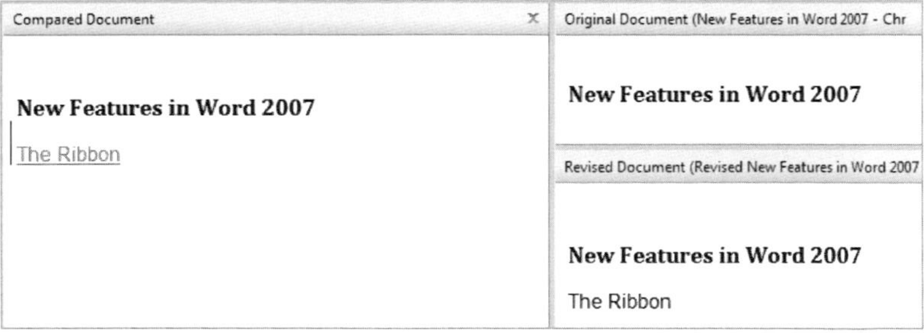

Figure 100

Mail Merge

Mail Merge is a quick way of merging information from one document into another allowing you to send personalised letters to groups of people or individuals by creating a main letter and a list of addresses that Word merges automatically. In order to do this two documents are needed, a Main document and a Data document.

Creating Letters using Mail Merge

1. Open a new document
2. Select

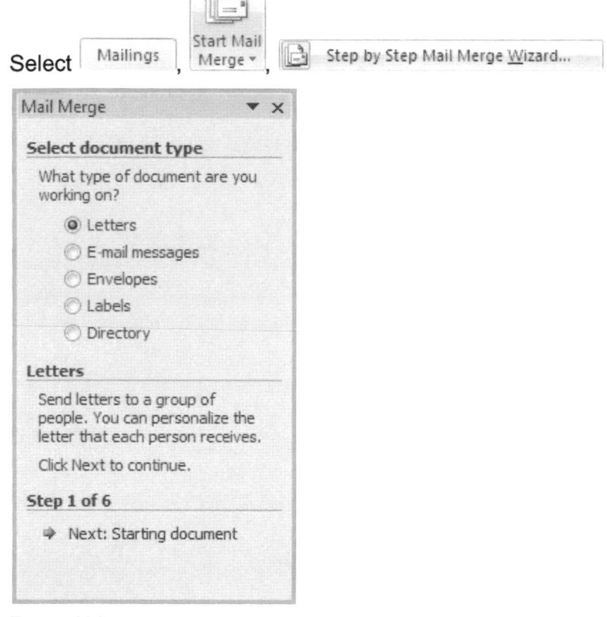

Figure 101

3. Select Letters from the document type
4. Click on Next: Starting Document to move to Step 2

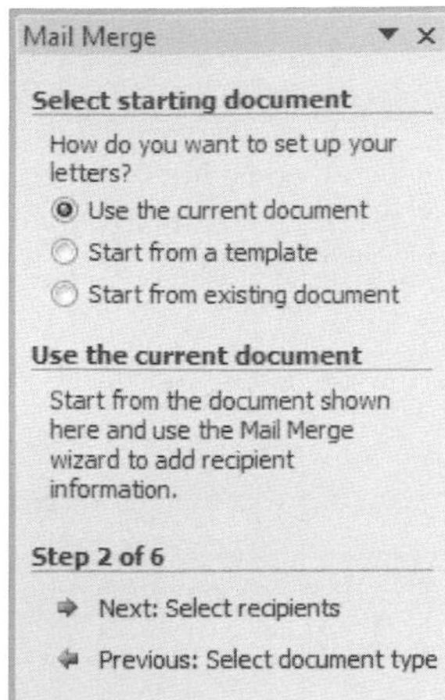

Figure 102

5. Select Use the current document
6. Click on Next: Select recipients to move to Step 3

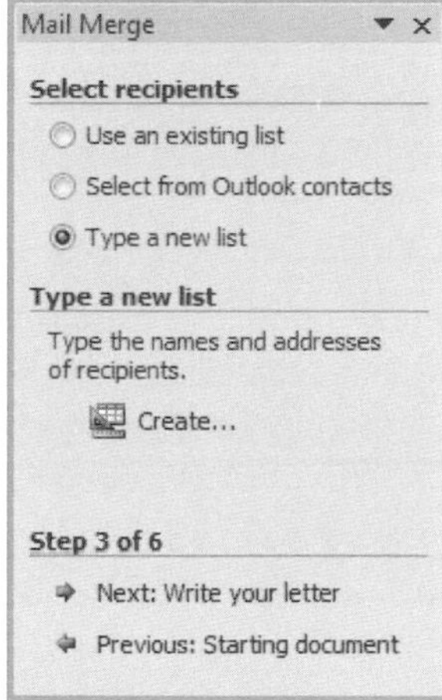

Figure 103

7. Choose Type a new list, click Create...

8. The New Address List dialog box appears

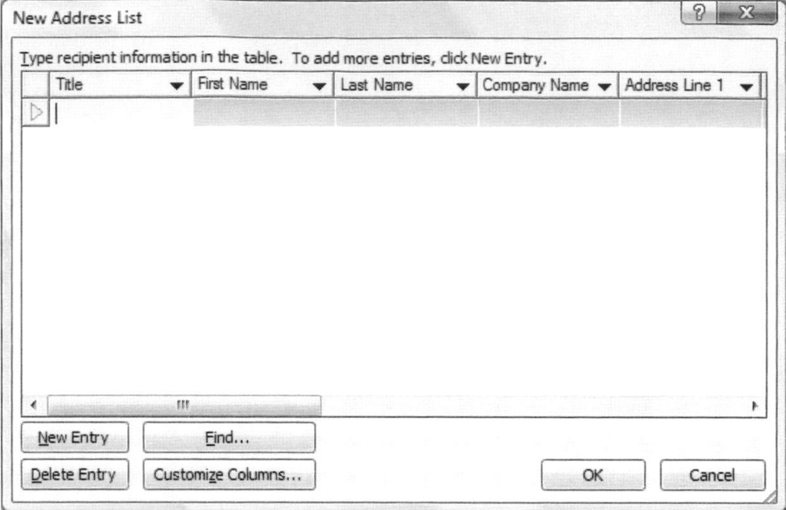

Figure 104

9. Select Customize Columns...

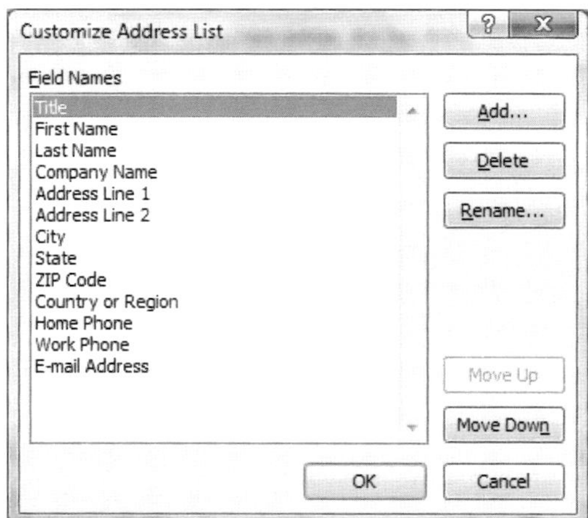

Figure 105

10. Edit Field Names as required

11. Select State, press Rename...

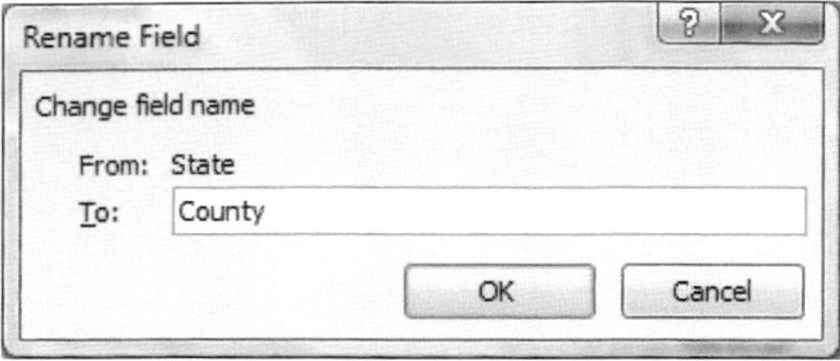

Figure 106

12. Type County, click OK, edit the Customise Address List as below

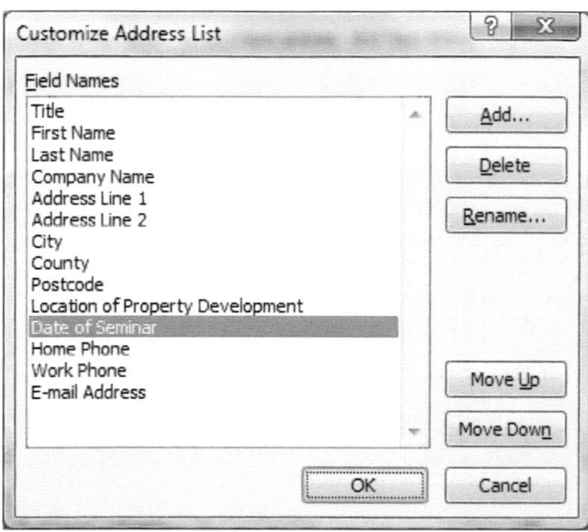

Figure 107

13. Add the following Field Names: Location of Property Development and Date of Seminar

14. Click OK to return to the New Address List

15. Enter the Address List as shown below

First Name	Last Name	Company Name	Address Line 1	Address Line 2	City	Post Code	Home Phone	Work Phone	Location of Property Development
Roy	Brown		7 Main Street		Sheffield	S60 2FF	0114 219 1234	0114 219 3456	Puerto Pollensa Mallorca
Marian	Longdale	Cottons Spa Limited	1 Chaffinch Road		Leeds	L1 2DF	0845 8900 7812	090 8900 7813	Alcudia Mallorca Spain
John	Bell	Knutsford Bridge Hotel	Macclesfield Lane		Lincoln	L6 9BV	0845 657731	01556 78921	Mondello Sicily Italy
Roger	Clarke	Northern Bell Company	Azric Drive		Bristol	BS32 1JK	01454 12234	01454 22564	Marbella Spain
Lucy	McDonald	Ullswater Lodge	11Ullswater Lane	Penrith	Cumbria	CA11 9OJ	01768 1234	01768 2345	Seville Spain

Figure 108

16. In the Field Name: Location of Property Development, enter a different location for each person in the Address List
17. In the Field Name: Date of Seminar, enter a date
18. Click OK, the Save Address List dialog appears
19. Save as Property Development Address List

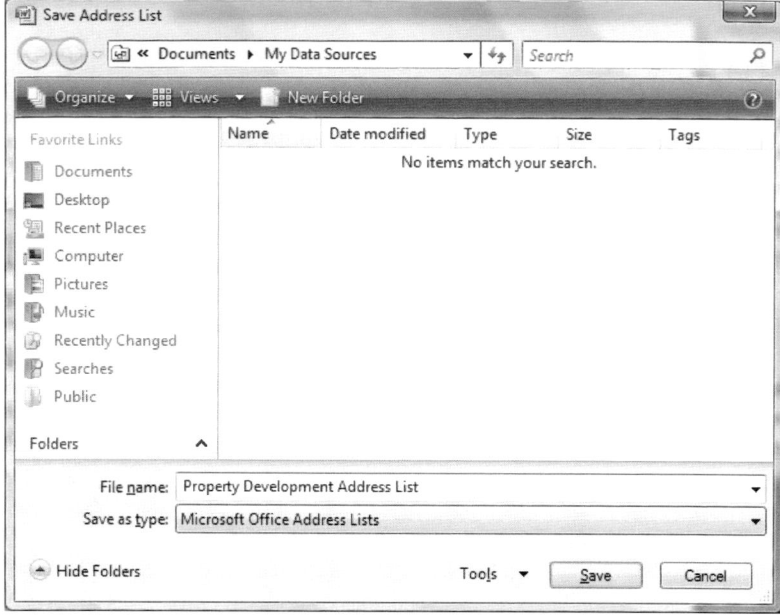

Figure 109

20. Click Save, the Mail Merge Recipients dialog check list appears

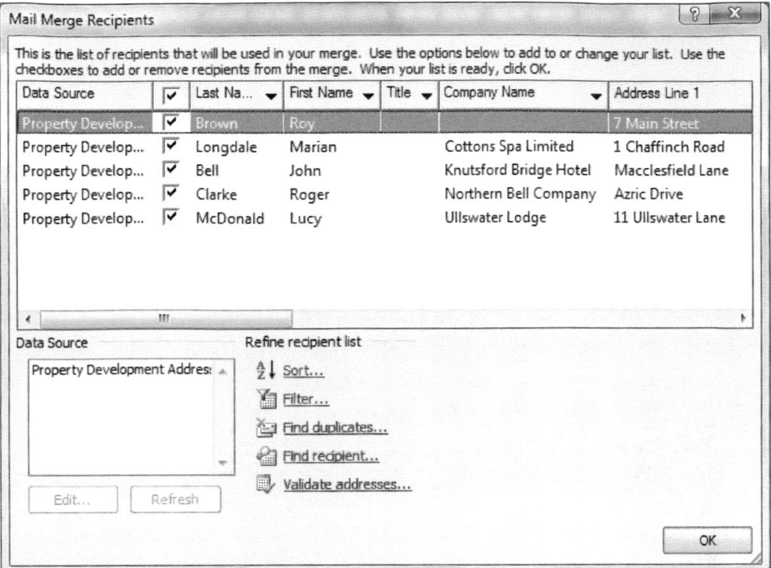

Figure 110

21. Check and edit the list as required
22. Select OK, click on Next: Write your letter to move to Step 4

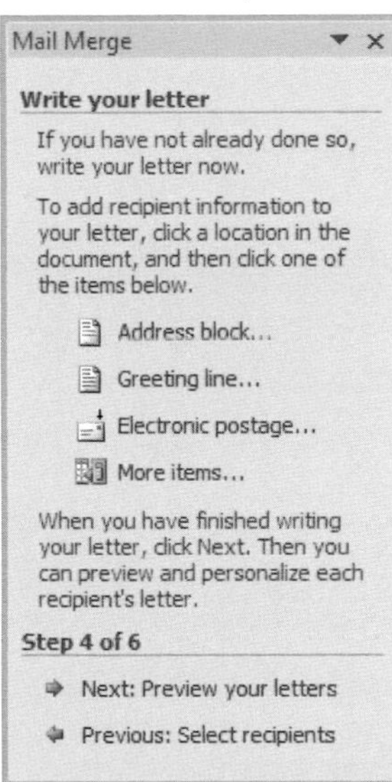

Figure 111

23. Type out the letter exactly as shown below

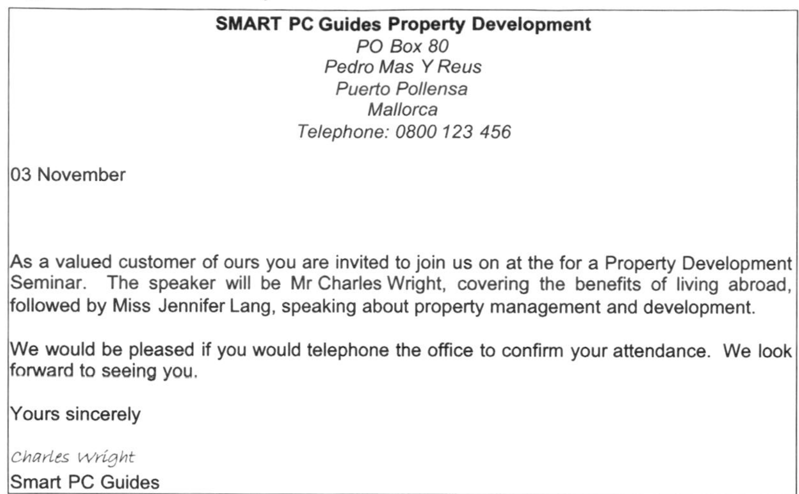

SMART PC Guides Property Development
PO Box 80
Pedro Mas Y Reus
Puerto Pollensa
Mallorca
Telephone: 0800 123 456

03 November

As a valued customer of ours you are invited to join us on at the for a Property Development Seminar. The speaker will be Mr Charles Wright, covering the benefits of living abroad, followed by Miss Jennifer Lang, speaking about property management and development.

We would be pleased if you would telephone the office to confirm your attendance. We look forward to seeing you.

Yours sincerely

Charles Wright
Smart PC Guides

Figure 112

24. Position the cursor where the address is to appear
25. Click on Address Block, the Insert Address Block dialog box appears

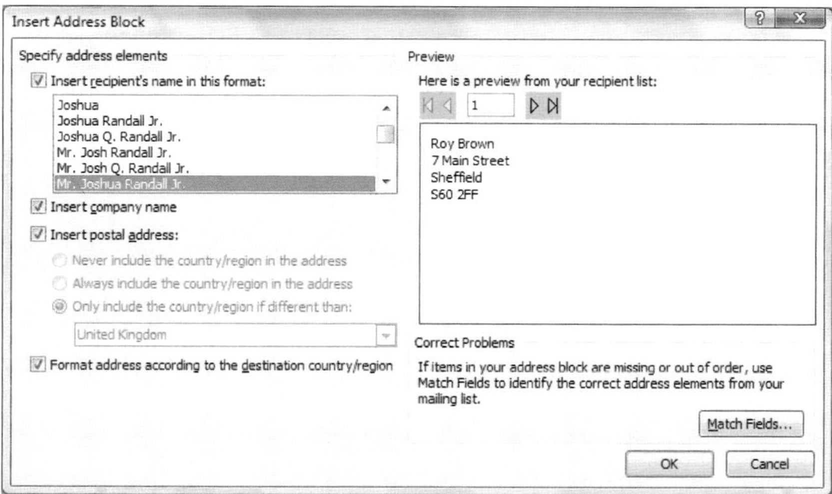

Figure 113

26. Select the required options, click OK
27. Position the cursor where the greeting line is to be placed

28. Select [Greeting line...], the Insert Greeting Line dialog box appears

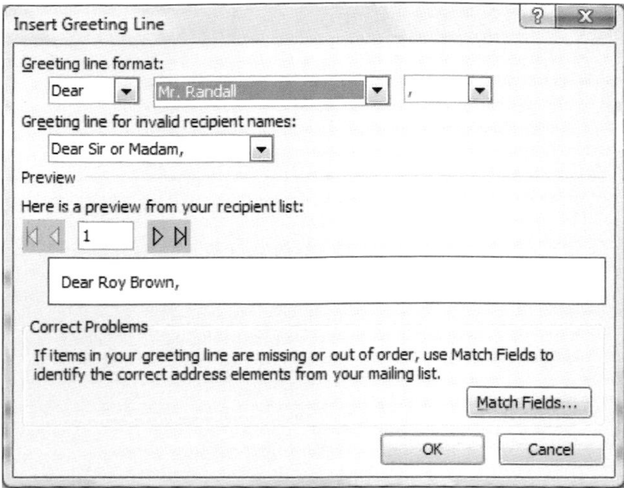

Figure 114

29. Select the required options, click [OK]
30. Place the cursor on the first line of the letter between the words **on** and **at**
31. Select [More items...], choose Date of Seminar
32. Click [Insert], press [Close]
33. Position the cursor between the words **the** and **for**
34. Select [More items...], select Location of Property Development
35. Click [Insert], press [Close]

36. Choose Next: Preview your letters to move to Step 5

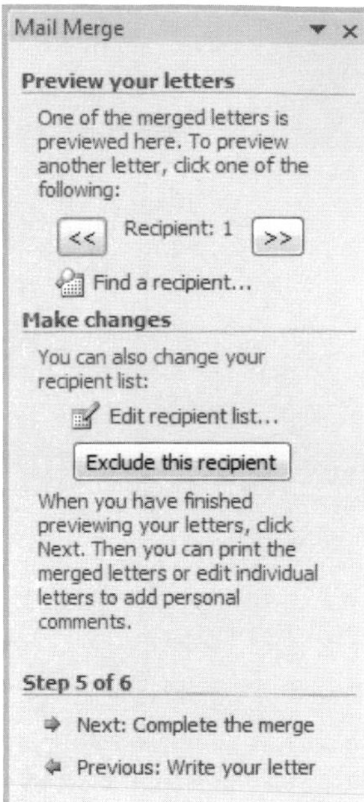

Figure 115

37. Step 5 enables you to preview and edit the final documents
38. Select Next: Complete the merge to move to Step 6

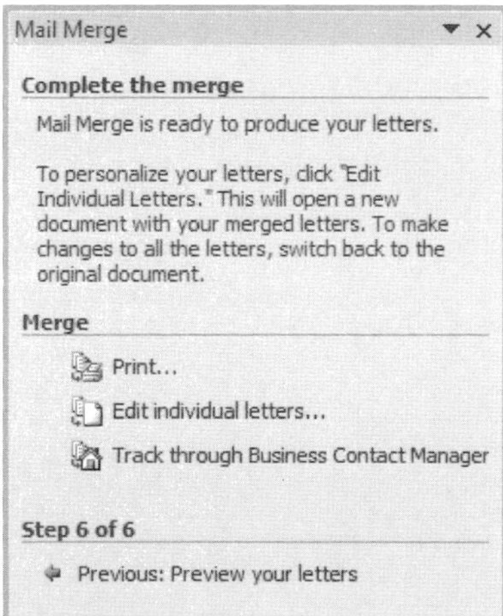

Figure 116

39. Select Edit individual letters
40. The Merge to New Document dialog box appears

Figure 117

41. Select **All**
42. Click OK the merged document appears on screen
43. Click the Office Button
44. Select Print, Print Preview Preview and make changes to pages before printing. to view the individual letters
45. Alternatively press Ctrl F2 to preview the pages
46. Press 

47. The Print dialog box appears, select OK

Creating Labels using Mail Merge

1. Open a new blank document
2. Select Mailings, Start Mail Merge, Step by Step Mail Merge Wizard..., choose Labels

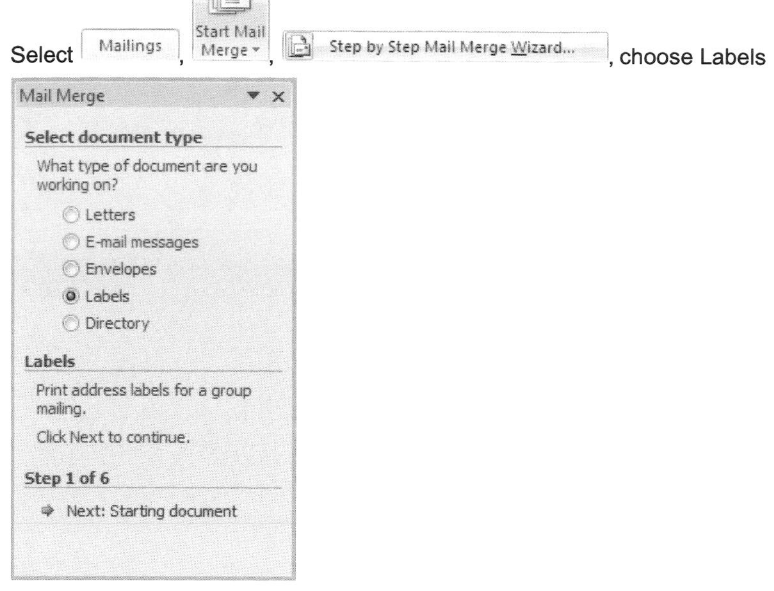

Figure 118

3. Select Next: Starting document to move to Step 2

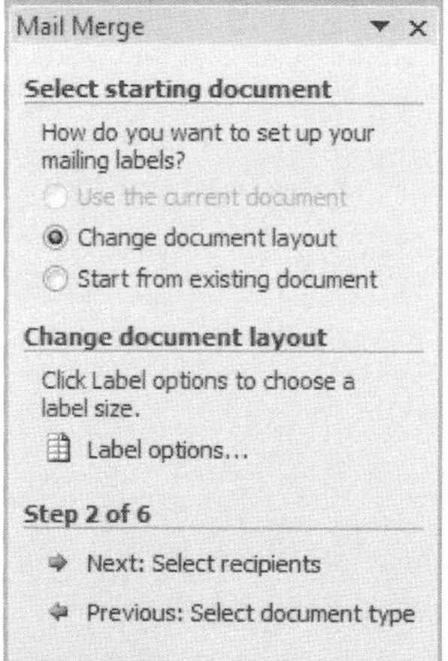

Figure 119

4. Select Change document layout, click Label options...
5. The Labels Options dialog box appears
6. Select the style of your labels, complete the options as shown below

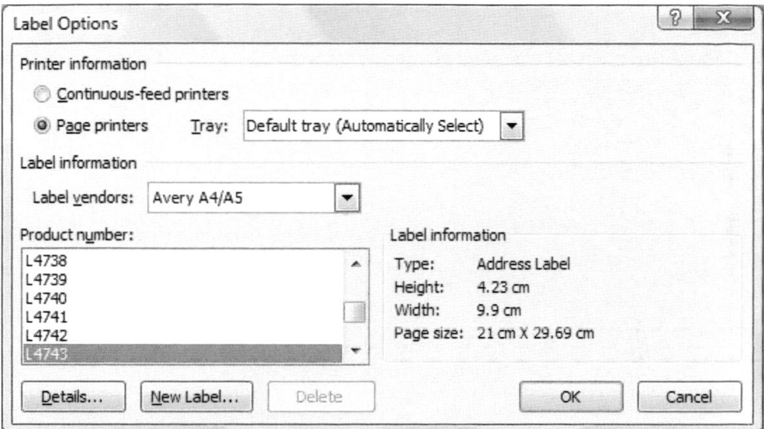

Figure 120

7. Click Details... to display more information on the label

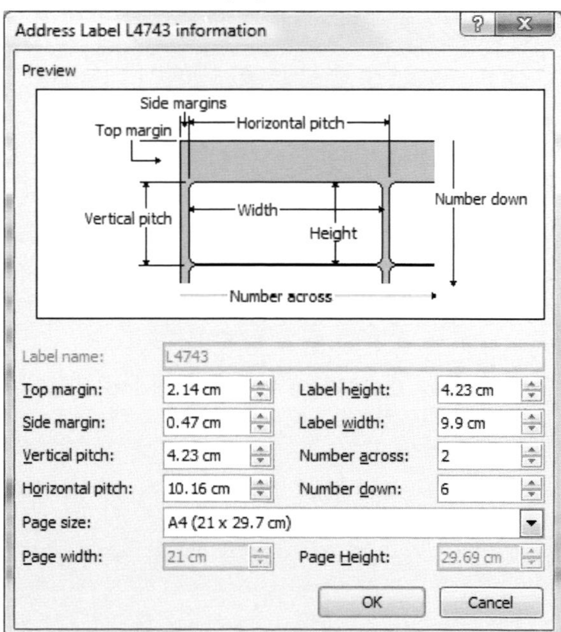

Figure 121

8. Press OK twice to return to the Mail Merge

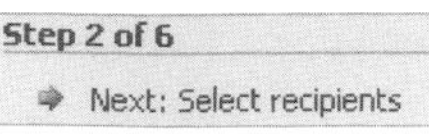

Figure 122

9. Press Next: Select recipients to move to Step 3

Figure 123

10. Click Use an existing list, select Use names and addresses from a file or a database. Browse...
11. Choose the file "Property Development Address List", press Open
12. To locate the document, click the left button on Documents
13. Double click with the left button on My Data Sources
14. Click the left button on Property Development Address List
15. Choose Open to display the Mail Merge Recipients dialog box

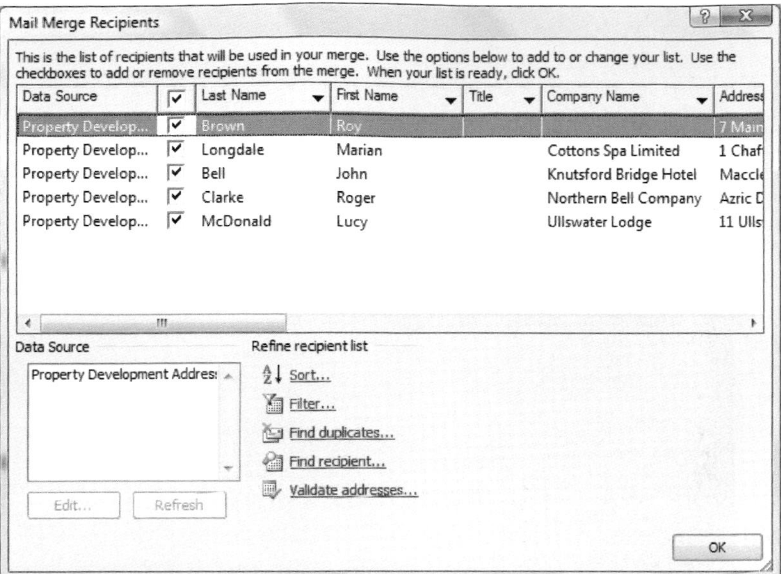

Figure 124

16. Deselect records not required by removing the ☑ with the left button
17. Press OK, click Next: Arrange your labels

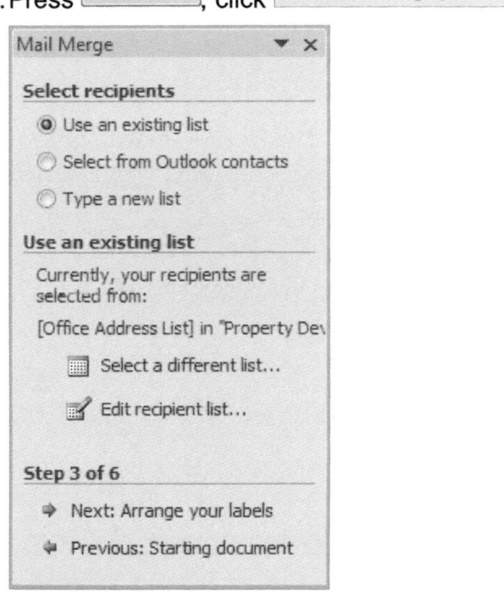

Figure 125

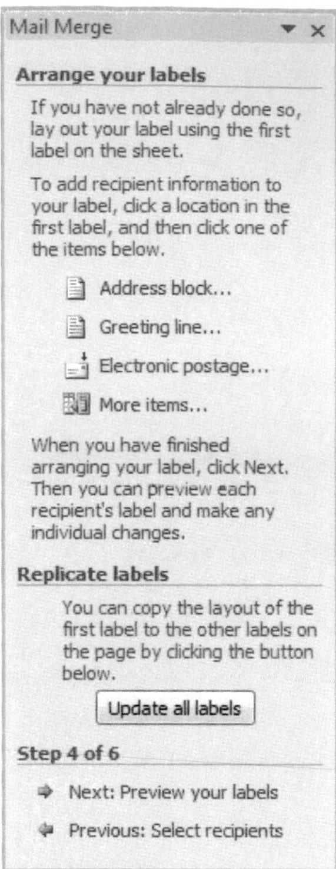

Figure 126

18. Select 

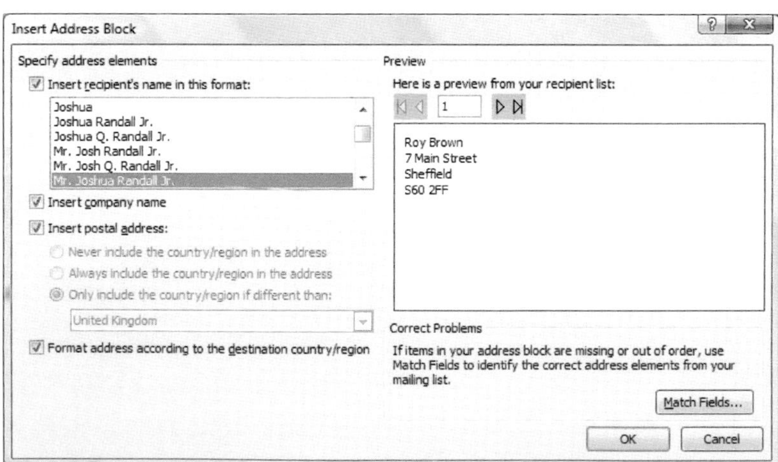

Figure 127

19. The Preview area displays the layout of your label
20. Choose OK
21. The flashing cursor appears after the **Address Block** in the first label
22. Select Update all labels

Figure 128

23. Select Next: Preview your labels

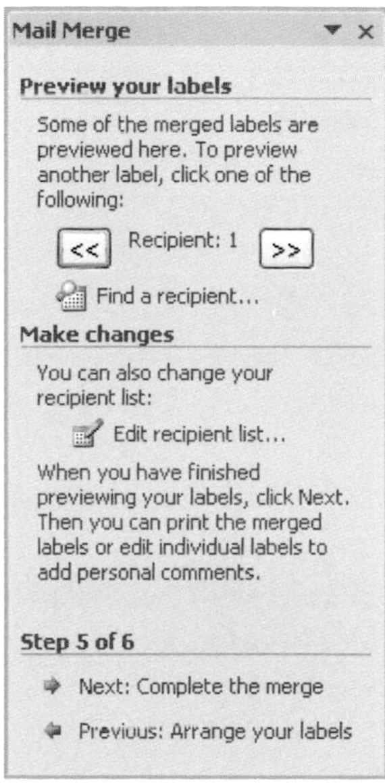

Figure 129

24. Choose Next: Complete the merge

Figure 130

25. Choose Edit individual labels... to merge the labels

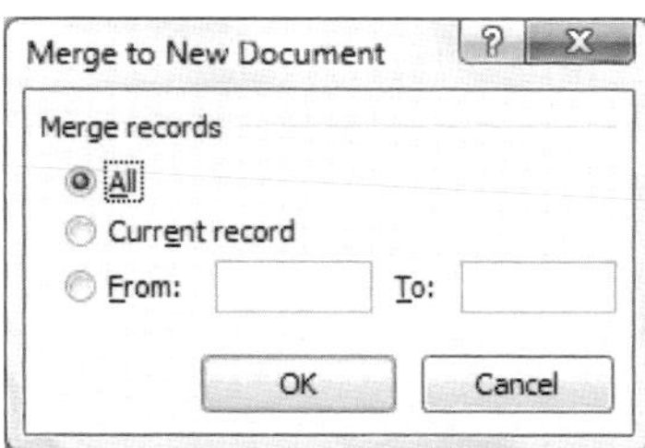

Figure 131

26. Select the appropriate option
27. Click  OK
28. Click the Office Button 
29. Select 

, to view the individual labels
30. Alternatively press Ctrl F2 to preview the pages
31. Press 

to display the print dialog box

Exercise 11: - Creating Labels

1. Select 

2. Create a labels address for your organisation
3. Reproduce the labels so they appear all on one page in a new document
4. Preview the results
5. Save the document as Company Labels

Templates

A template is a means of creating a document that is consistent allowing such documents as letters, faxes and memos to be used with preset styles and formatting. When a new document is created based on a template it is used as the foundation for the new document.

Templates are saved to the Normal general area; however, it is possible to create a new tab for an organisation in the templates area that allows company templates to be quickly identified.

To Save a Document as a Template

1. Open the document to be saved as a template
2. Click the Office Button
3. Select Save As, Word Template Save the document as a template that can be used to format future documents.
4. Name the template in the File **name** area
5. Ensure Save as type: Word Template is selected, click New Folder
6. In Name, type Smart PC Guides Templates, press Enter
7. The Smart PC Guides folder is opened

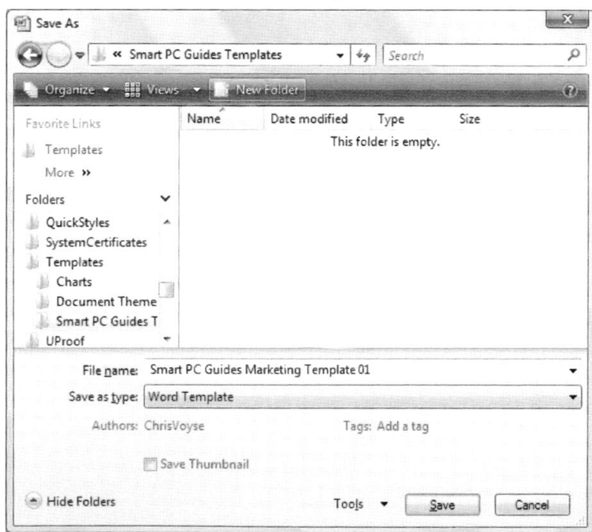

Figure 132

8. Save the template as Smart PC Guides Marketing Template 01

View a Template

1. Click the Office Button
2. Select New, My templates...
3. Choose the Smart PC Guides Template Tab

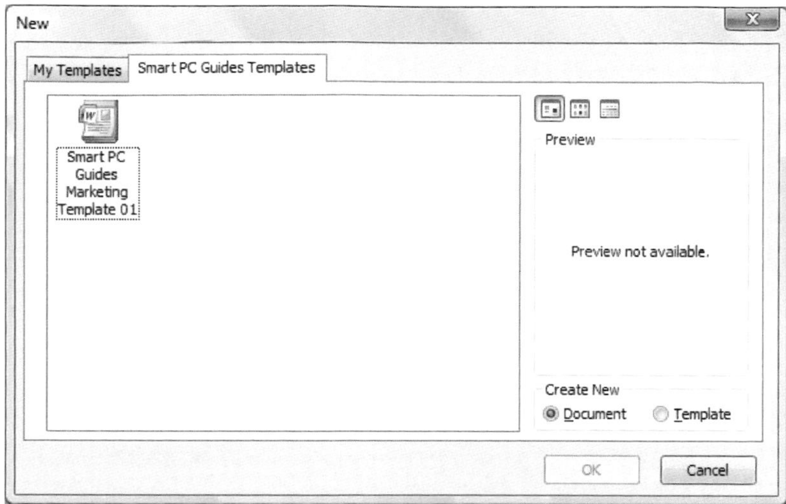

Figure 133

4. Select the Smart PC Guides Marketing Template 01
5. A new document based on the template is created
6. Click OK

Open and Amend an Existing Template

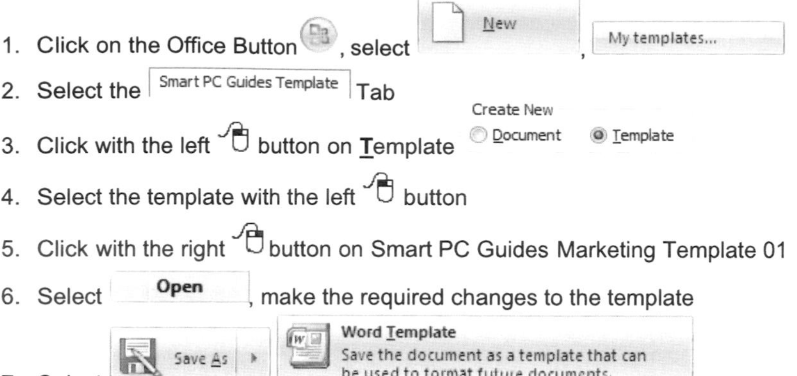

1. Click on the Office Button, select New, My templates...,
2. Select the Smart PC Guides Template Tab
3. Click with the left button on Template
4. Select the template with the left button
5. Click with the right button on Smart PC Guides Marketing Template 01
6. Select Open, make the required changes to the template
7. Select Save As, Word Template — Save the document as a template that can be used to format future documents.
8. The Save As dialog box appears displaying the Template folders
9. Double click the left button, open the Folder Smart PC Guides Templates

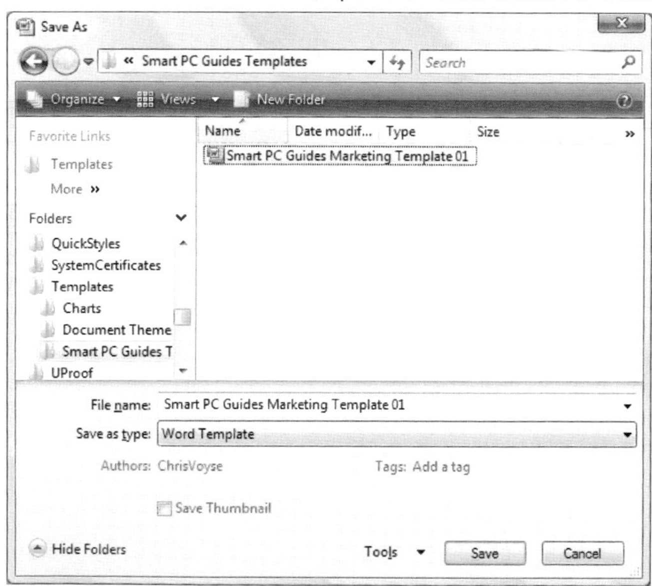

Figure 134

10. Click the left button on Smart PC Guides Marketing Template 01
11. Select Save, the following dialog appears

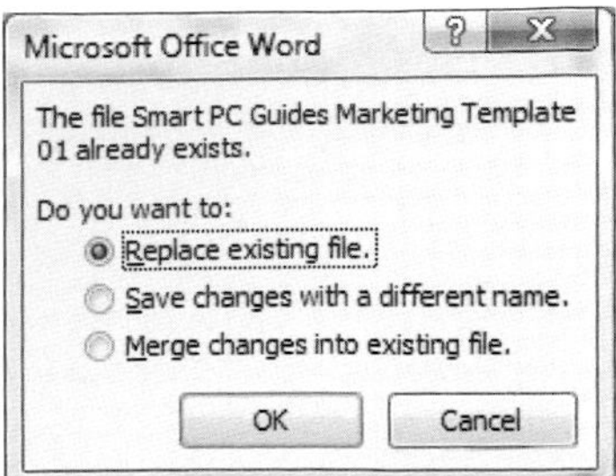

Figure 135

12. Select **R**eplace existing file
13. Choose OK, the changes have been updated in the template
14. Open a new document based on the template to view the changes

Section 3: Expert Level Objectives

- Outline View
- Create a Master Document
- Designing a Form in Word
- Introduction to Macros
- Watermarks
- Hyperlinks
- Creating Newspaper Columns
- Linking Information with other MS Products
- Inserting Pictures and Graphics
- The Drawing Toolbar
- Working with Text Boxes
- Create Footnotes and Endnotes
- Shortcut Keys

Note: If you are working in Windows XP instead of Windows Vista, dialog boxes may look different but function in a similar way.

Using Outline View

Outline View allows a document's structure to be seen when the document has been created using Styles and Formatting. The document can be collapsed or expanded to view headings and specific parts of the document to allow quick and easy re-organisation by moving, copying or dragging headings and text. If the document contains a Table of Contents and changes have been made to the document, this can be updated in Outline View.

The Outline Commands

1. Open a new document
2. Select View, Outline from the Document Views Grouping
3. The Outlining Commands appear

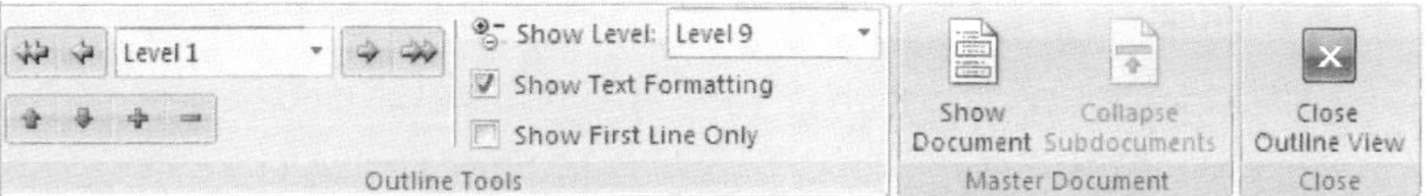

Figure 136

Outlining an Existing Document

1. Open a new document, create the following text using Styles and Formatting
2. Construct the document using Heading Styles 1-3 and a numbering list
3. Save the document as Working in Outline View

Note: The document that has been created below contained additional text that has been collapsed identified by the ⊕ sign. The document you have created will contain a ▭ sign.

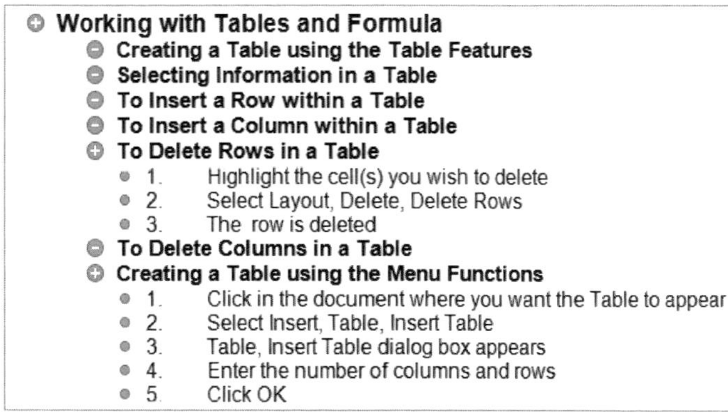

Working with Tables and Formula

- **Creating a Table using the Table Features**
- **Selecting Information in a Table**
- **To Insert a Row within a Table**
- **To Insert a Column within a Table**
- **To Delete Rows in a Table**
  - 1. Highlight the cell(s) you wish to delete
  - 2. Select Layout, Delete, Delete Rows
  - 3. The row is deleted
- **To Delete Columns in a Table**
- **Creating a Table using the Menu Functions**
  - 1. Click in the document where you want the Table to appear
  - 2. Select Insert, Table, Insert Table
  - 3. Table, Insert Table dialog box appears
  - 4. Enter the number of columns and rows
  - 5. Click OK

Figure 137

4. Select Outline View
5. Click with the left button on the word Formula in the title heading
6. Press the key to the end of the document
7. As you scroll the Heading Style Level changes to the defined styles

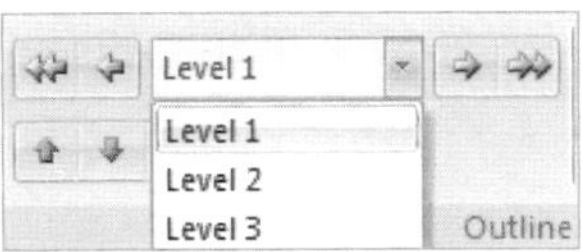

Figure 138

8. Select Show Level: Level 2 from the Outlining Tools Command
9. The document is collapsed showing Heading Styles 1 and 2
10. Click with the left button on the to display the hidden item
11. Press the to collapse the selected item
12. Alternatively double click on the plus sign with the left button to collapse or expand the section
13. Select Show Level: All Levels to display all the items

Promote and Demote Information

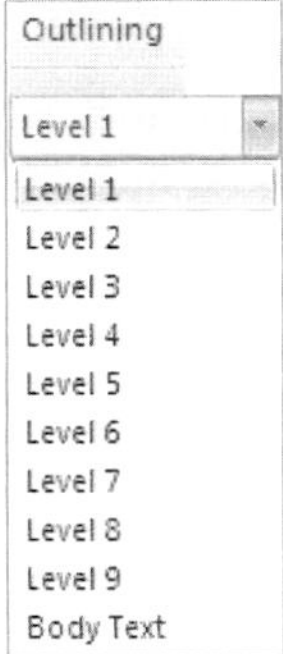

Figure 139

1. Place the cursor in a heading style, click the Promote to Heading 1 icon
2. The style is automatically changed to Heading 1
3. Select the Demote to Body Text icon to change the style to Body Text or the Normal default style
4. The Promote icon moves forward to the next highest level
5. The Demote icon moves backwards to the next lowest level
6. Alternatively select the Outline icon Level 2

Move Information in Outline View

1. Select Move Up to move information upwards to a new location
2. Choose Move Down to move information downwards
3. Select Expand to expand selected items
4. Choose Collapse to collapse the selected item

Note: All collapsed information is kept with the heading when being moved to a new location in Outline View.

Exercise 12: - Working with a Table of Contents

Table of Contents

Monday	2
Briefing at 10:00	2
Tuesday	3
Performance Review at 15:00	3
Wednesday	4
Progress Meeting 09:30	4
Thursday	5
Staff Appraisal at 14:15	5
Friday	6
Company Car New Criteria	6

1. Generate the Table of Contents shown above
2. Select References, Update Table
3. Scroll to the beginning of the table
4. Change Briefing at 10:00 to Normal Style
5. Change Company Car New Criteria to Heading Style 3
6. Click Update Table
7. Select Update entire table

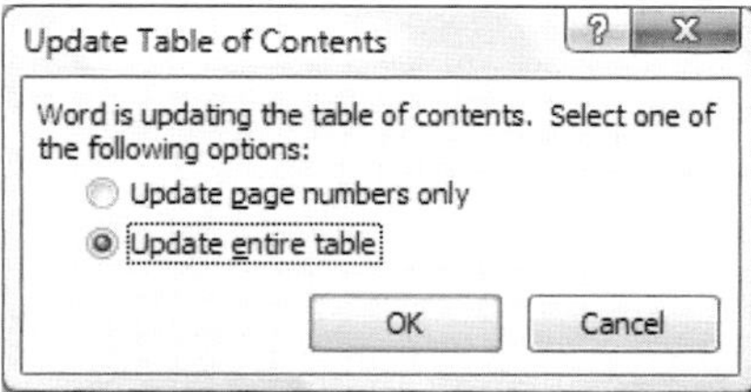

8. Click OK to view the updated Table of Contents
9. Close and save the document as Generating a Table of Contents

Create an Outlined Numbered List

The Outline Number feature automatically indents lists of items at different levels.

1. Open a new document
2. Select Home, choose Multilevel List from the Paragraph Grouping

Figure 140

3. Choose the option highlighted below from the List Library gallery

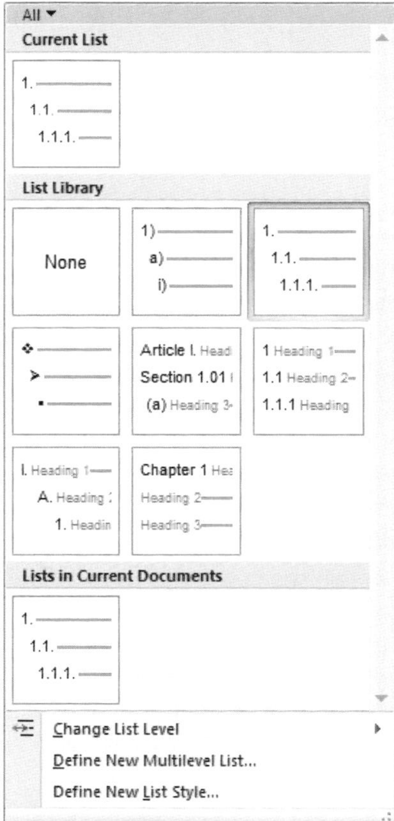

Figure 141

1. Microsoft does the work for you
    1.1. No Business can work without the technology of today
        1.1.1. This is never truer, than when it comes to needing a reliable word processing system.........................
        1.1.2. The busy office requires all of the tools of today's technology to help it work effectively............
2. Accounting at the touch of a button
    2.1.|

Figure 142

4. Type out the text above
5. Press Enter and Tab to move in a level
6. To move back a level press Shift and Tab

Master Documents

A Master Document is used to organise and maintain long documents by dividing it into Subdocuments that are managed by links to the Master Document.

Creating a Master Document

1. Create a folder named Master Documents
2. Open a new document
3. Select Outline View, the Outlining commands appears

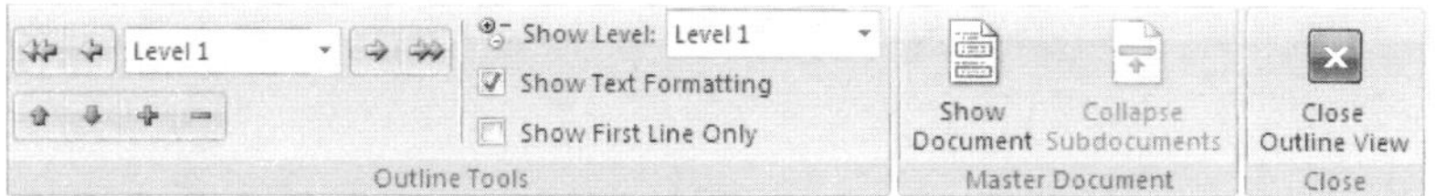

Figure 143

4. Select Level 1 from the Outlining commands, this represents Heading Style 1
5. Type Demonstration of Master Documents, press Enter
6. Select Body Text, this represents Normal style

"The following example demonstrates the creation of Master Documents, inserting subdocuments, moving subdocuments in the Master Document, adding a new subdocument to the Master Document and deleting a subdocument"

Figure 144

7. Press Enter
8. Switch to Print Layout View, click on the Show Styles Window icon
9. Return to the Outline View, the Styles window is displayed
10. Select Level 1, type Chapter 1, press Enter

11. Select Level 2, type Inserting a Subdocument, press Enter
12. Create Chapters 2 and 3
13. Highlight Chapter 1 and the Normal body text associated with it
14. Click with the left button on Show Document

15. The Master Document Grouping is expanded

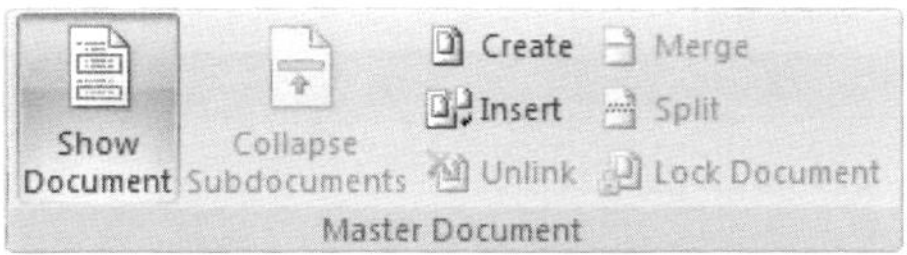

Figure 145

16. Click on the Create Subdocument icon Create
17. Repeat the steps to create subdocuments for the other Chapters
18. Save the document as Demonstration of Master Documents in the Master Documents Folder
19. Close the document

Opening a Subdocument

1. Open the folder Master Documents Folder
2. Open the subdocument Chapter 1
3. Add some additional text, save and close the document

Inserting a Subdocument

1. Open a new document, select View, Outlining
2. Select Level 1, type Chapter 4, press Enter
3. Select Level 2 Heading Style 2, type Adding a New Document, press Enter
4. Select the Body Text Level Normal Style, type the following text

“This demonstrates creating a new document and adding it to the Master Documents.

Figure 146

5. Save the document as Chapter 4 in the Master Documents folder
6. Close the document

7. Re-open the document named Demonstration of Master Documents

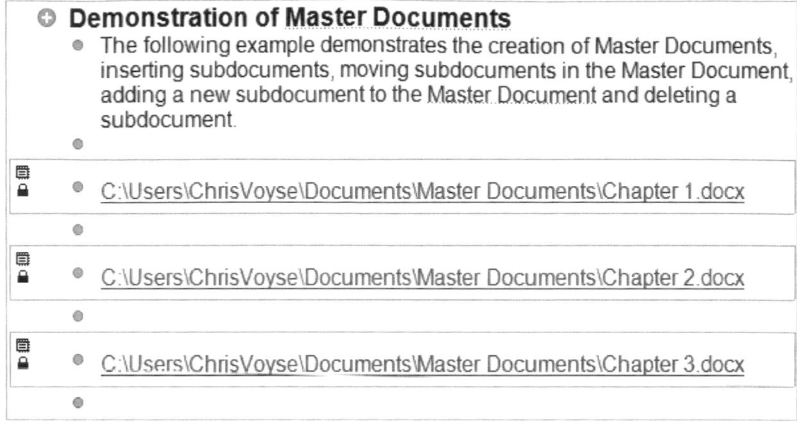

Figure 147

8. The Subdocuments appear in a collapsed form
9. Click on 

10. Ensure the cursor is positioned at the end of the document
11. Click with the left button on Insert Subdocument icon Insert
12. The Insert Subdocument dialog box appears
13. Select the document Chapter 4, click Open
14. Chapter 4 is incorporated into the Master Document
15. Save and close the Master Document

Moving a Subdocument

1. Open the document Demonstration of Master Documents, select the subdocument to be moved
2. Click and hold down the left button on the subdocument icon positioned in the top left hand corner of the subdocument box

Figure 148

3. Drag the subdocument to a new location

Note: Double click on the subdocument icon to open an individual document, to return to the Demonstration of Master Documents, close that particular individual document.

Delete a Subdocument

1. Expand the Master Document, select the subdocument to be deleted
2. Click on the Subdocument icon to highlight the document
3. Press Delete

Lock and Unlock Subdocuments

If another person tries to work on a subdocument that is already in use, the subdocument is automatically locked to others. Password protection could be applied to the subdocument; this feature is covered later in the Smart PC Guide.

Using the Form Commands

Text can be inserted into documents using Form Fields that are created by Drop-Down Form Fields or Check Box Form Fields. This is useful when a form is to be filled out on screen allowing Status Bar Text and Help Text Fields to assist users to complete the form electronically. Forms can be designed with a variety of formats using text and numbers and by setting the maximum length of each field or size.

Exercise 13: - Creating a Form using the Form Commands

Training Needs Analysis Form

Name:

Employers Name:

Daytime Telephone Number:

Mobile Number:

Contact Address:

Address Line 2:

Town/City:

Postcode:

Country:

Select a Course of Interest:

Microsoft Word	***Microsoft Excel***	***Microsoft PowerPoint***
Foundation	*Foundation*	*Foundation*
Intermediate	*Intermediate*	*Intermediate*
Expert	*Expert*	*Expert*

Tick the following areas of interest

Voice Recognition

Facial Recognition

Handwriting Recognition

1. Open a new document
2. Using a table create the Training Needs Analysis Form shown above
3. Save the form as a template named Training Needs Analysis Form

Inserting Text Form Fields

1. Click on the Office Button
2. Select Word Options, choose Popular
3. Place a tick on Show Developer tab in the Ribbon
4. Press OK
5. Select the Developer Tab Developer
6. Choose Legacy Tools from the Controls Grouping
7. Select the Form Field Shading icon
8. To deselect the shading, click on the Form Field Shading icon
9. Click with the left button where the Text Form Field is to appear
10. Choose abl from the Legacy Tools menu
11. Create the Form Fields for the rest of the form
12. Centre align the Text Form Fields
13. Save the form

Inserting Check Box Form Fields

1. Select the Developer Tab
2. Choose Legacy Tools from the Controls Grouping
3. Select the Form Field Shading icon
4. To deselect the shading, click on the Form Field Shading icon
5. Click with the left button where the Check Box Form Field is to appear
6. Choose from the Legacy Tools menu
7. Create the Check Box Form Fields for the rest of the form
8. Centre align the Check Box Form Fields
9. Save the form

Training Needs Analysis Form

Name:	{FORMTEXT}
Employers Name:	{FORMTEXT}
Daytime Telephone Number:	{FORMTEXT}
Mobile Number:{ FORMCHECKBOX}	{FORMTEXT}
Contact Address:	{FORMTEXT}
Address Line 2:	{FORMTEXT}
Town/City:	{FORMTEXT}
Postcode:	{FORMTEXT}
Country:	{FORMTEXT}
Select a Course of Interest:	{FORMDROPDOWN}

Microsoft Word	***Microsoft Excel***	***Microsoft PowerPoint***
Foundation	*Foundation*	*Foundation*
Intermediate	*Intermediate*	*Intermediate*
Expert	*Expert*	*Expert*

Tick the following areas of interest

Voice Recognition	{FORMCHECKBOX}
Facial Recognition	{FORMCHECKBOX}
Handwriting Recognition	{FORMCHECKBOX}

Figure 149

Customising the Text Form Fields

The Text Form Fields can be customised using a variety of options such as regular text, number, date, current date, current time, calculations, length, field settings and help keys.

1. Click on the first Text Form Field to be customised
2. Select the Developer Tab, choose Properties from the Controls grouping
3. The following dialog box appears

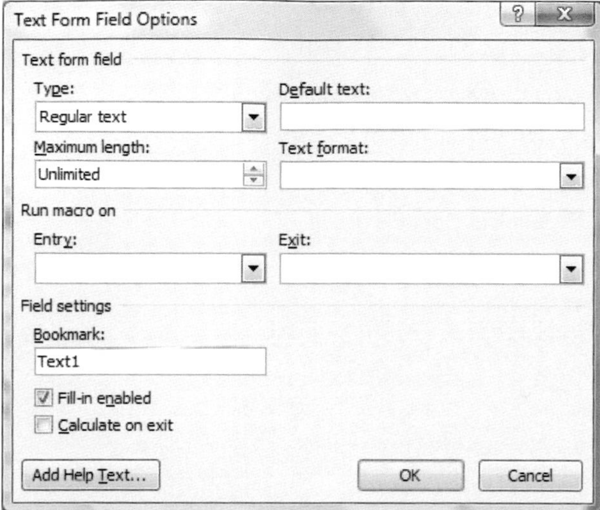

Figure 150

4. In the Type box, click on the arrow, select Regular text
5. Click on Add Help Text...

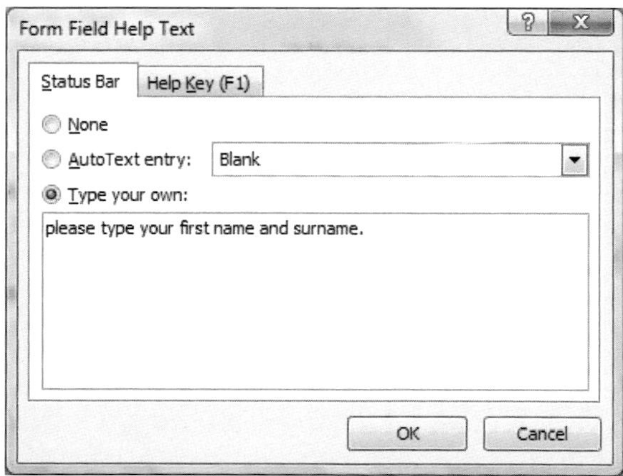

Figure 151

6. In the Type your own box, type your first name and surname
7. Select Help Key (F1) Tab

8. In the Type your own box, type your first name and surname
9. Click OK twice
10. Repeat the process to customise the other Text Form Fields
11. Save the form

Note: If using numbers in a Text Form Field, select the numbering option and select a maximum length required. The Number Format lets you choose several different formats to control how the number will be displayed.

Customising the Check Box Form Fields

1. Highlight the Check Box Form Field for Mobile Number
2. Select Properties from the Controls grouping
3. The Check Box Form Field Options dialog box appears

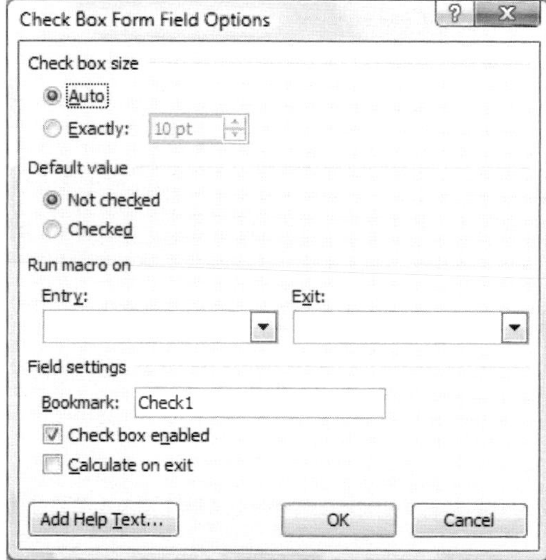

Figure 152

4. Click on Add Help Text...

5. Select the **S**tatus Bar Tab, type the text as shown below

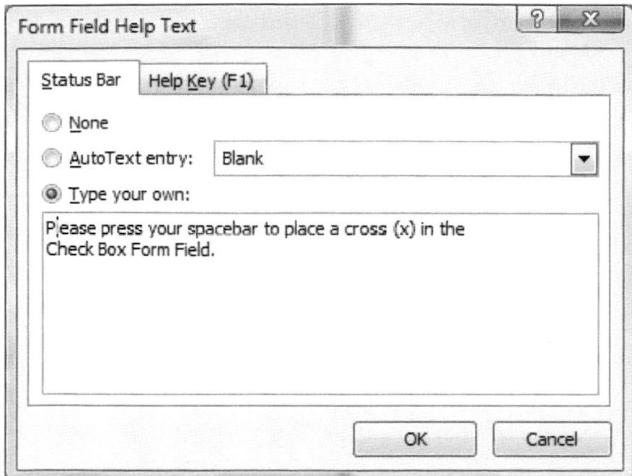

Figure 153

6. Select the Help Key (F1) Tab type the following text as shown below

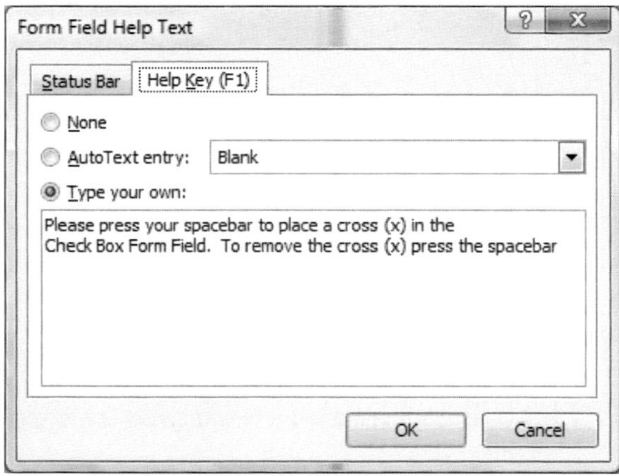

Figure 154

7. Click OK twice

Protecting Forms

A document or template that contains Form Fields must be protected in order for the fields to be activated. When the form is ready to be protected

1. Select 

2. The Restrict Formatting and Editing Task Pane appears

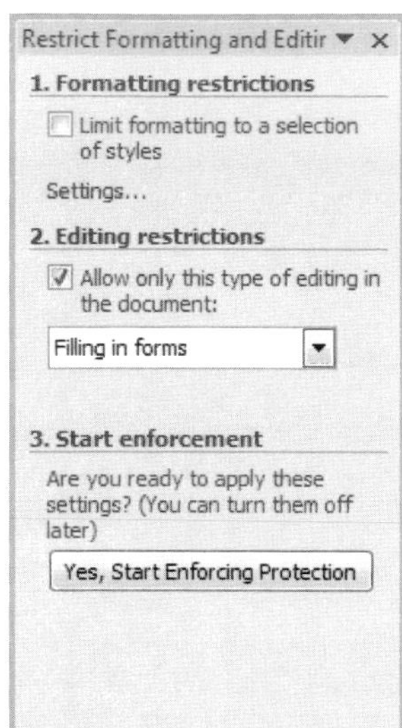

Figure 155

3. Click with the left button on Design Mode to switch off the Design Mode
4. Alternatively press Alt L D M to switch the Design Mode on or off
5. Tick editing restrictions, choose Filling in forms
6. Press Yes, Start Enforcing Protection, the Start Enforcing Protection dialog box appears

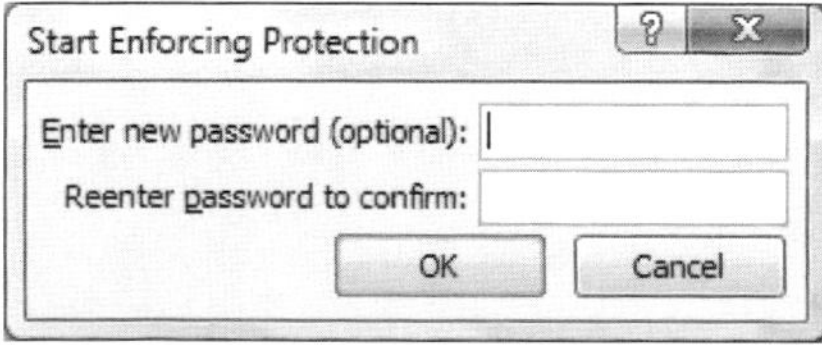

Figure 156

7. Press OK, the document is protected

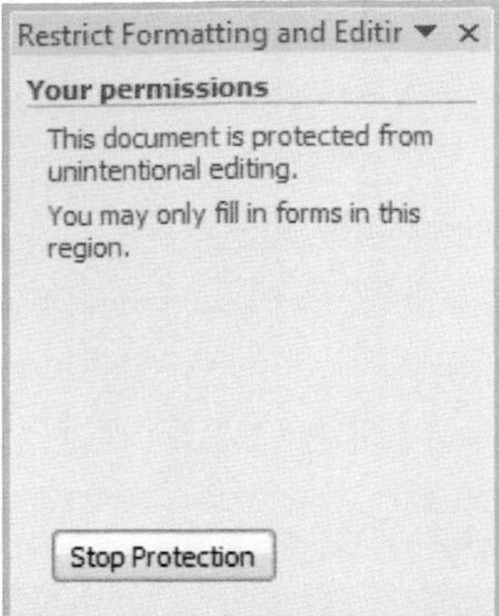

Figure 157

8. To unprotect the document click with the left button on Stop Protection
9. If a password has been set the following dialog box appears

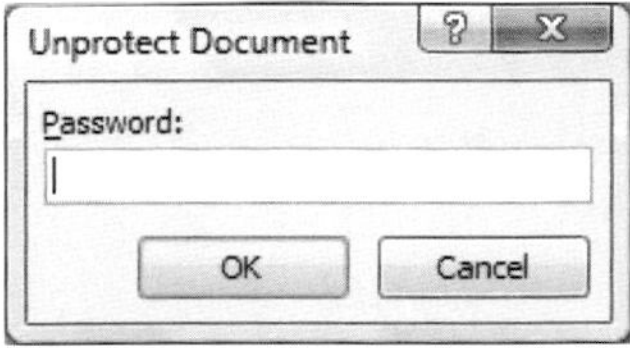

Figure 158

10. Press OK, the document is unprotected

Note: A form can be protected without using passwords however if a user clicks on unprotect the form can be altered. When using passwords remember passwords should be more than 8 characters in length using letters, numbers and symbols. WRITE DOWN THE PASSWORD USED AND KEEP IT IN A SECURE PLACE TO ENABLE ACCESS TO BE GAINED WHEN NECESSARY.

Define AutoText Entries

1. Open a new document
2. Type out and right align your address, highlight the address
3. Select Insert, Quick Parts, Save Selection to Quick Part Gallery...
4. The Create New Building Block dialog box appears
5. Complete the box as shown below

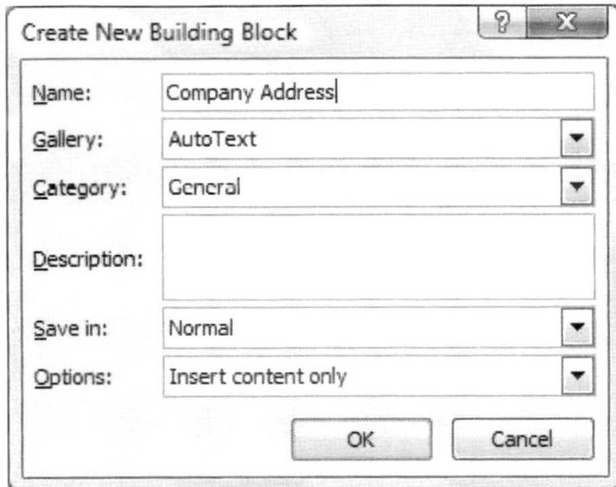

Figure 159

6. Click OK
7. Select, 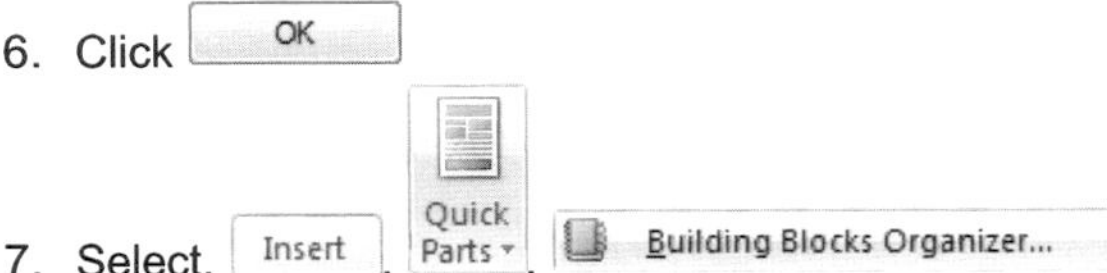

8. Alternatively press Alt N Q B to access the building block organiser

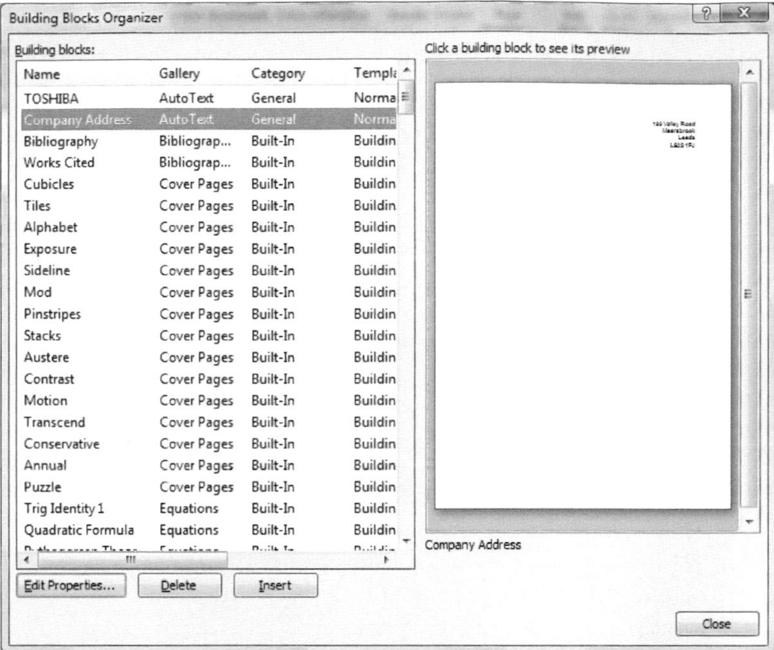

Figure 160

9. Click [Insert], the address is inserted in the document

Create Date Fields

1. Working in the same document, place the cursor where the date is to appear
2. Select Insert, Quick Parts, Field...
3. Alternatively press Alt N Q F
4. Select **C**ategories: choose Date and Time

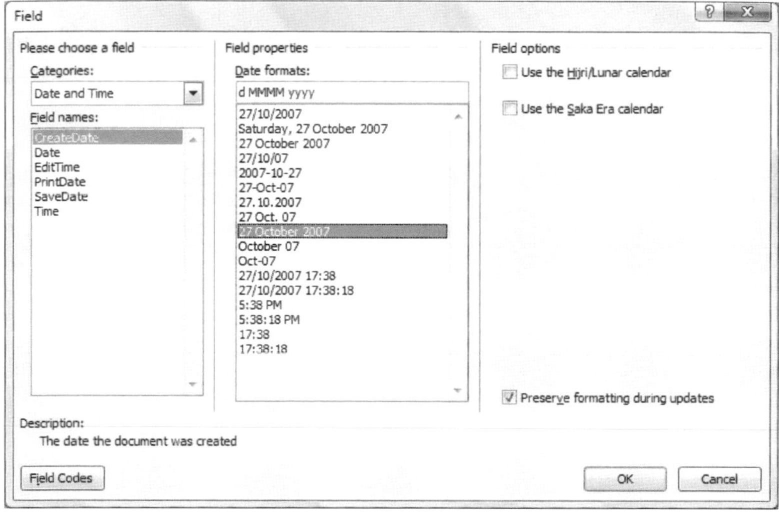

Figure 161

5. In **D**ate formats: select the required format, click OK
6. The date appears in the document, press Alt F9 to view the field code

{CREATEDATE \@ "d MMMM yyyy" * MERGEFORMAT}

Figure 162

7. Press Alt F9 to return to the document, save the document

Note: An alternative way to create a date field is to click Ctrl F9, type between the brackets {CREATEDATE \@ "d MMMM yyyy" *MERGEFORMAT}, click Alt F9, press Alt F9 to revert back to the field code.

Using the AutoText List

1. Click in the document where you want a salutation to appear
2. Select Insert, Quick Parts, Field...
3. Select Categories, choose (All)
4. In Field names, choose AutoTextList, click in the New value: box
5. Type the salutation required

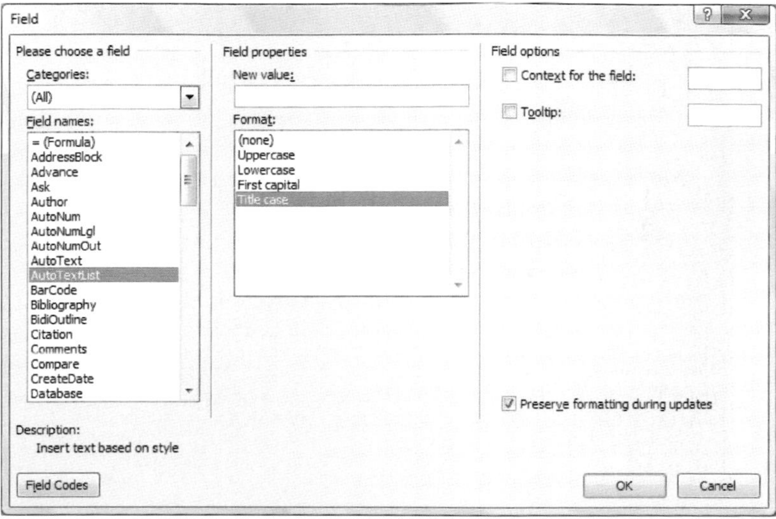

Figure 163

6. In the Format box, select Title case
7. Choose Field Codes to view the Advanced field properties

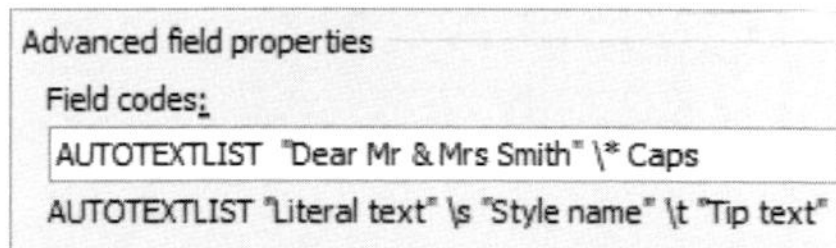

Figure 164

8. Click OK, the following field appears in the document

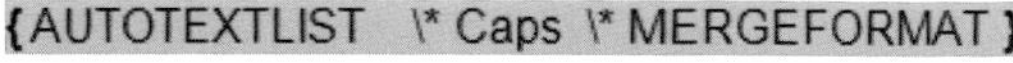

Figure 165

9. Press Alt F9, Dear Mr & Mrs Smith appears in the document
10. Save the changes to the document

Using the ASK Field

The ASK Field is used at the beginning of a document to instruct the user to input data at other locations in the document in conjunction with Bookmarks.

1. Ensure the cursor is positioned where text is to be inserted
2. Select Insert, Quick Parts, Field...
3. In Field names: choose Ask

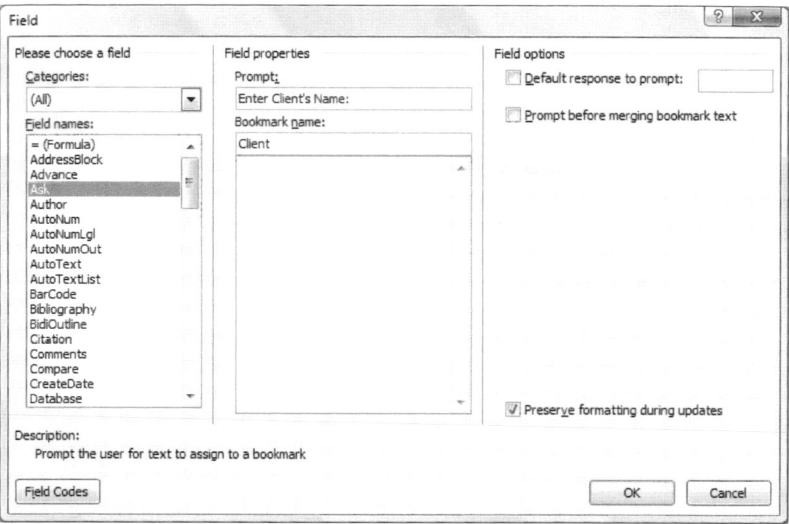

Figure 166

4. In Prompt: type, Enter Client's Name
5. In Bookmark name type Client, select Field Codes
6. Click OK, the following prompt appears

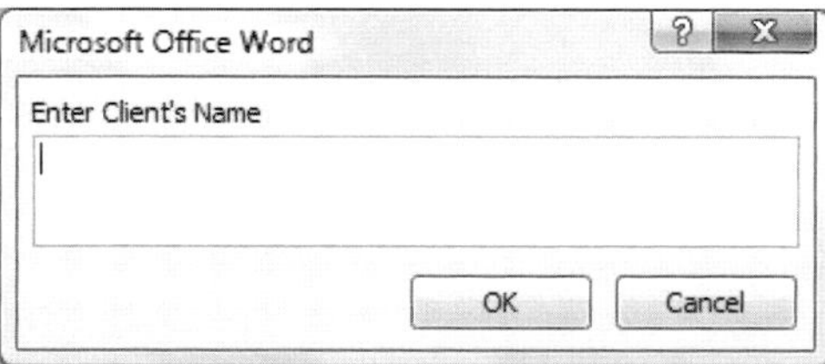

Figure 167

7. In the Enter Client's Name box type, ABC Limited, press OK

8. Type the following paragraph starting, This contract…..

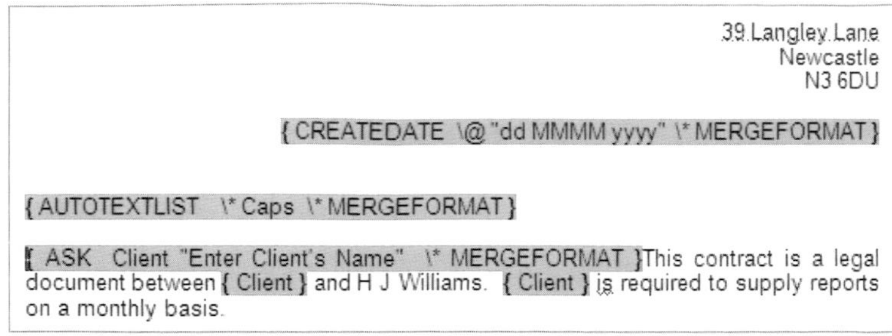

39 Langley Lane
Newcastle
N3 6DU

{ CREATEDATE \@ "dd MMMM yyyy" * MERGEFORMAT }

{ AUTOTEXTLIST * Caps * MERGEFORMAT }

{ ASK Client "Enter Client's Name" * MERGEFORMAT }This contract is a legal document between { Client } and H J Williams. { Client } is required to supply reports on a monthly basis.

Figure 168

9. After the word "between", press Ctrl F9
10. Type Client between the brackets as above
11. Repeat the process as shown above after the first sentence
12. Select Ctrl A to highlight the whole document, press F9
13. Enter Client's Name dialog box appears

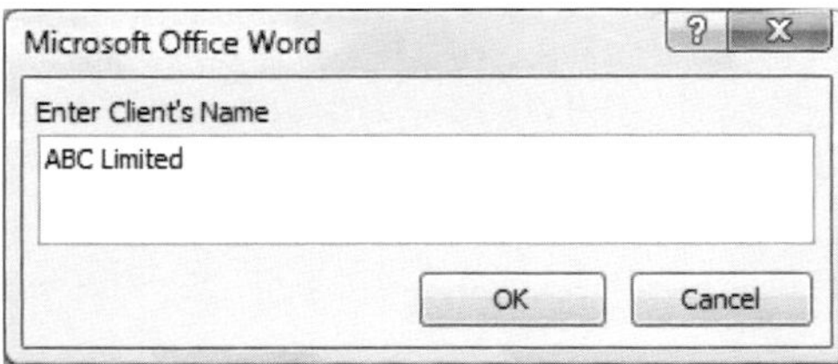

Figure 169

14. Click OK, press Alt F9 to view the text on screen

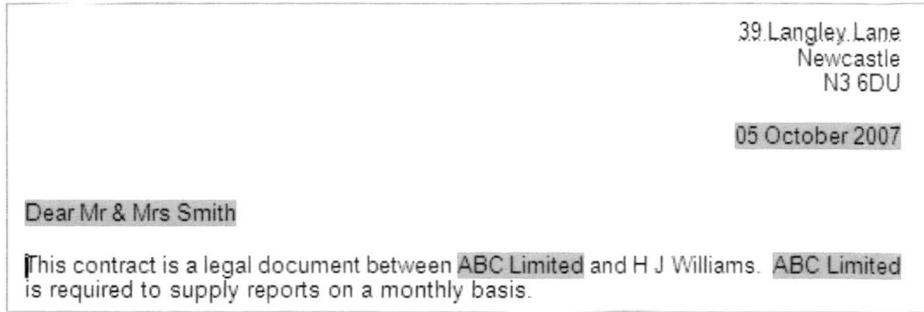

39 Langley Lane
Newcastle
N3 6DU

05 October 2007

Dear Mr & Mrs Smith

This contract is a legal document between ABC Limited and H J Williams. ABC Limited is required to supply reports on a monthly basis.

Figure 170

15. Preview and save the document

Exercise 14: - Using Fill-in Fields

The Fill-in Field requires the user to input information at a particular location in the document where the field has been created.

1. Open the document used in the previous section

2. Select Insert, Header
3. Centre align
4. Select Insert, Quick Parts, Field...
5. In Field names: choose Fill-in

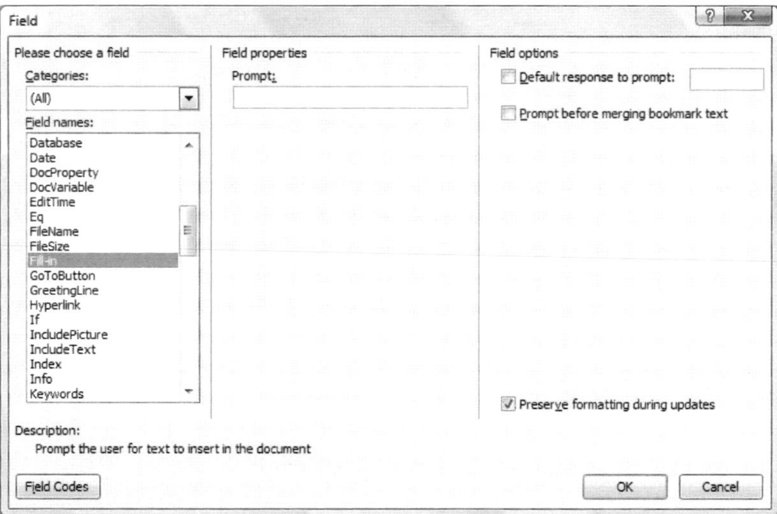

6. In the Prompt: field; type "Enter the company name"
7. Select Field Codes

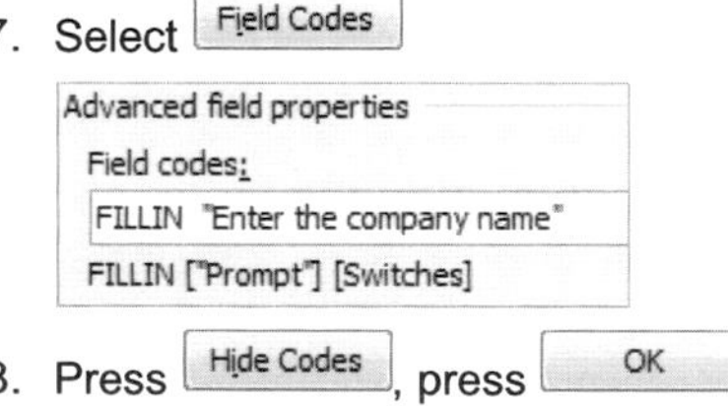

8. Press Hide Codes, press OK

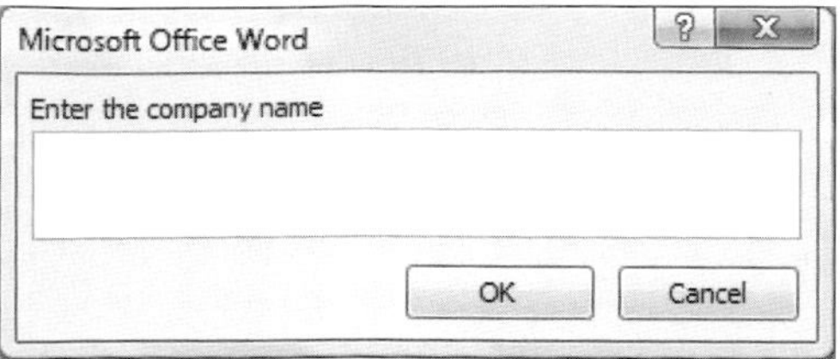

9. Click OK, the Fill-in field is displayed

   { FILLIN "Enter the company name" * MERGEFORMAT }

10. Create Fill-in fields for:

    { FILLIN "What position do you hold in the company?" * MERGEFORMAT }

    { FILLIN "What is your telephone number?" * MERGEFORMAT }

11. Create a closing using AutoText
12. Select Alt F9 to view the text
13. Save the document as a template, close the document
14. Create a new document based on the created template
15. Complete the Fill-in Fields as appropriate
16. Select Alt F9 to display the text, preview and save the document

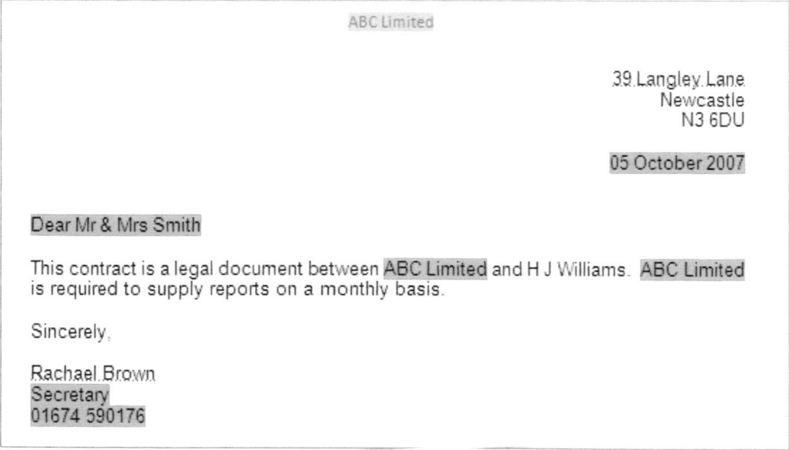

ABC Limited

39 Langley Lane
Newcastle
N3 6DU

05 October 2007

Dear Mr & Mrs Smith

This contract is a legal document between ABC Limited and H J Williams. ABC Limited is required to supply reports on a monthly basis.

Sincerely,

Rachael Brown
Secretary
01674 590176

Macros

A macro allows you to perform repeated tasks that combine multiple commands and automates complex tasks. Macros can be assigned to a specific document or generated from a template. Before recording a Macro prepare, plan and practice the steps to ensure that the commands function correctly.

Record a Macro

1. Open a new document
2. Select View, Macros, Record Macro...

3. Alternatively press Alt W M R
4. The Record Macro dialog box appears

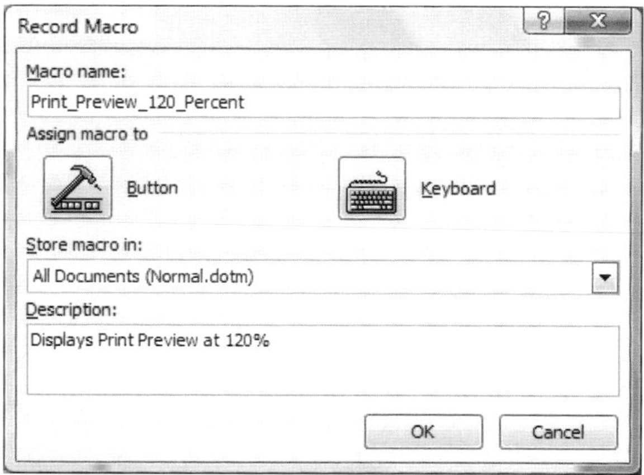

Figure 171

5. Complete the dialog box as shown above, click OK
6. Back in the document the mouse pointer has a tape icon attached
7. Press Ctrl F2 to display print preview
8. The status of the macro is recording
9. Click on the Zoom icon to display the zoom dialog box

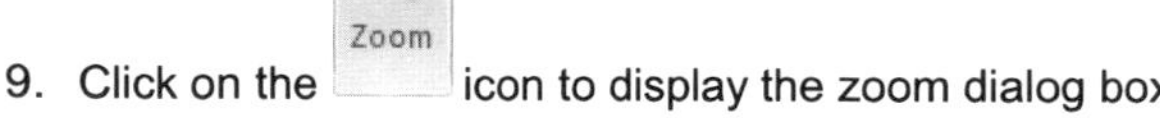

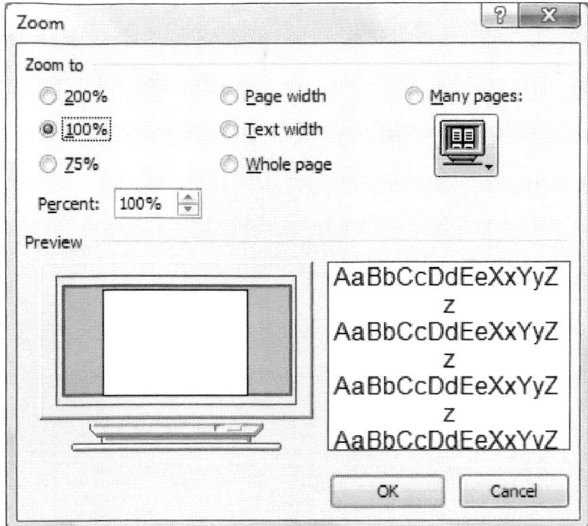

Figure 172

10. Type 120 in the P**e**rcent area or use the arrow keys to increase the percentage Percent: 120%,
11. Select OK, the page is zoomed to 120%
12. Click the left button on the Stop Recording icon in the Status Bar

Assigning a Macro to a Shortcut Key

1. Select 
2. The Record Macro dialog box appears
3. Define the **M**acro name as Print_Preview_143_Percent
4. **S**tore the macro in All Documents (Normal.dotm)
5. Click the left button to assign the macro to the keyboard
6. The Customise Keyboard dialog box appears

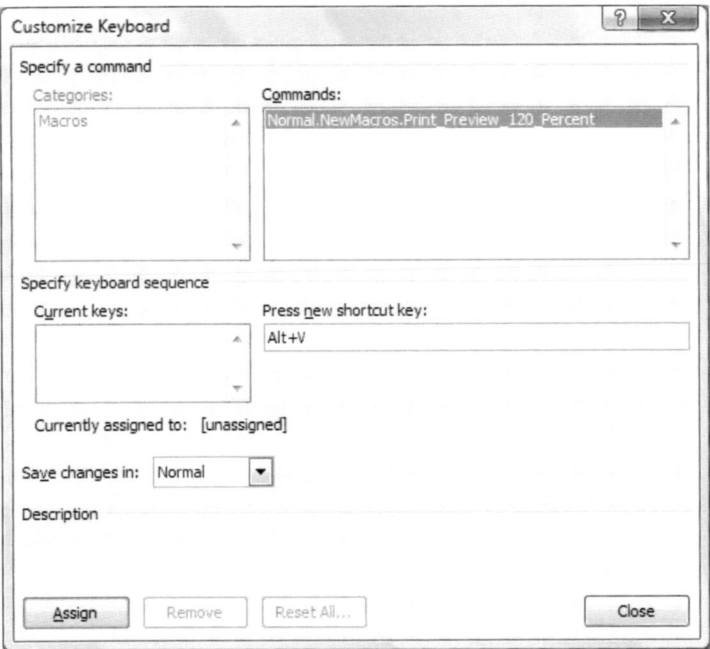

Figure 173

7. The flashing cursor appears in the press **n**ew shortcut key area
8. Hold down Alt and press V, the **Alt+V** states currently [unassigned]
9. Click Assign, press Close
10. The Status Bar shows that a macro is recording identified by the Macro Recording icon

Using the Menu Bar to View and Edit a Macro

1. Select 

2. Alternatively press Alt W M V

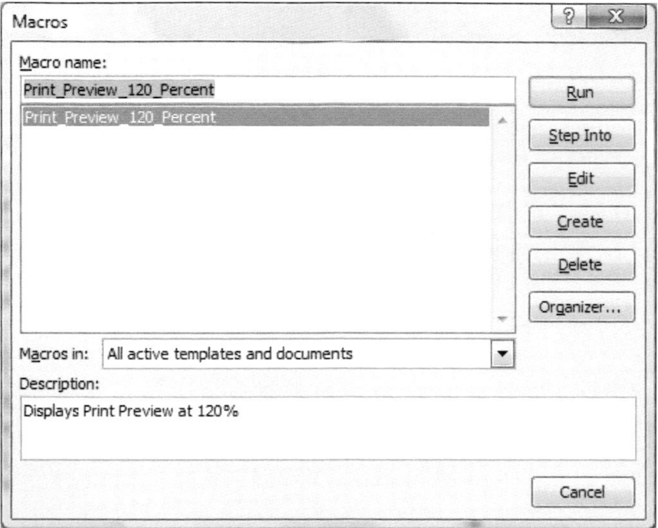

Figure 174

3. Click on Print_Preview_120_Percent, select Edit
4. The Normal - NewMacros (Code)] screen appears

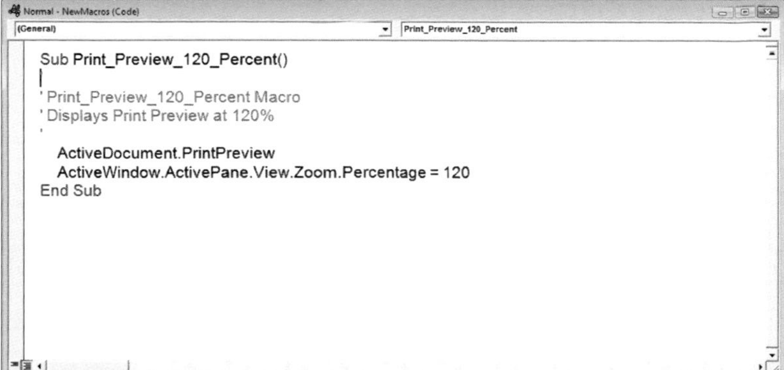

Figure 175

5. Press Ctrl F

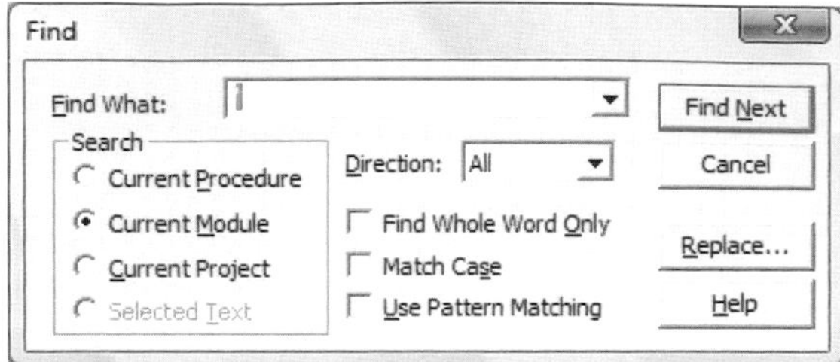

Figure 176

6. In the Find What area, type 120, click on Find Next, choose Cancel
7. Ctrl H displays the Replace dialog box

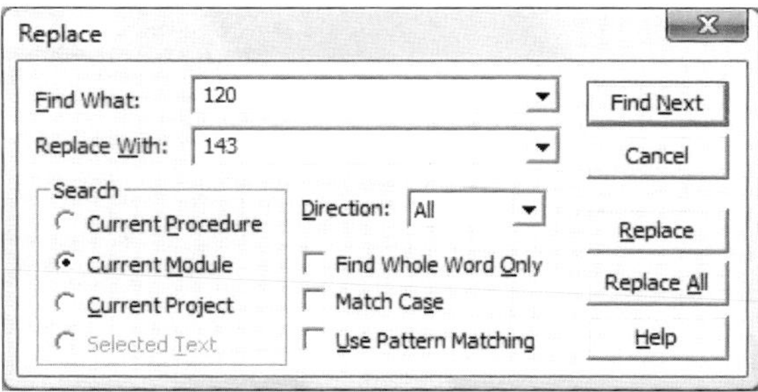

Figure 177

8. Type the criteria as shown above, click on Replace
9. The criteria is changed to 143, the following prompt appears

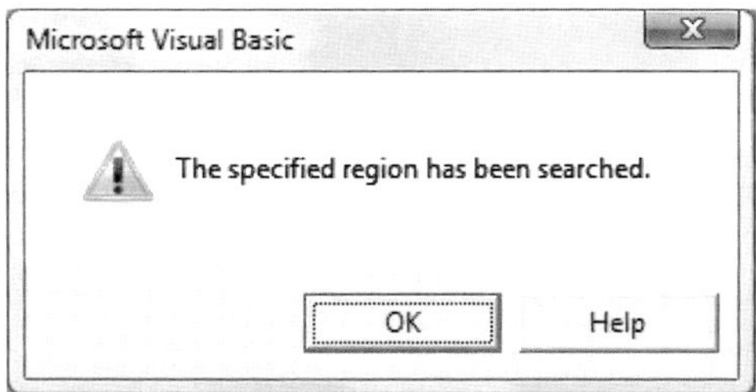

Figure 178

10. Click OK to close the dialog box, choose Cancel
11. Alternatively press Alt F8 to display the Macro dialog box
12. Click Run the Macro Name and view is 143%

Deleting a Macro

1. Open the document that contains the macro to be deleted
2. Select 

3. Alternatively press Alt F8 to display the Macro dialog box

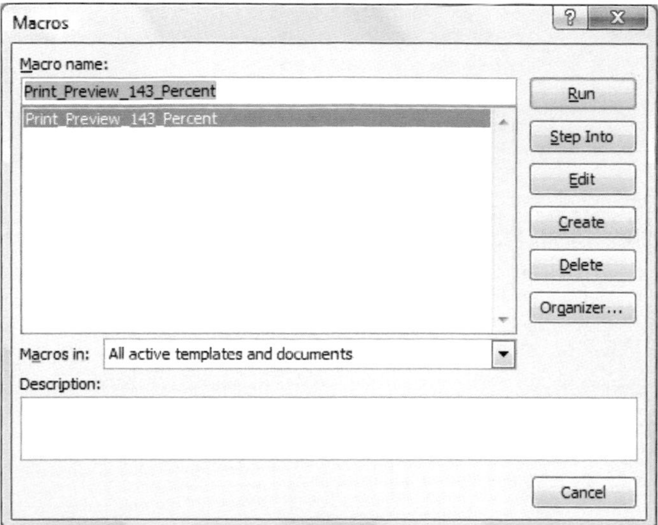

Figure 179

4. Press Delete

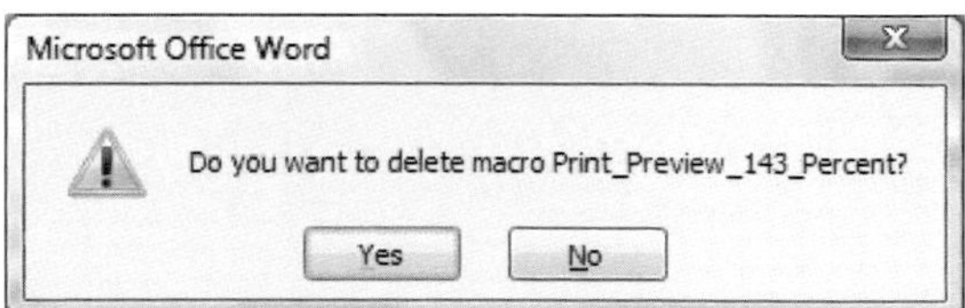

Figure 180

5. Select Yes, the Macro is deleted

Exercise 15: - Generate a Table of Contents Macro

Table of Contents

Monday 2
Briefing at 10:00 2
Tuesday 3
Performance Review at 15:00 3
Wednesday 4
Progress Meeting 09:30 4
Thursday 5
Staff Appraisal at 14:15 5
Friday 6
Company Car New Criteria 6

1. Open a new document
2. Generate the Table of Contents above using Styles Heading 1-3
3. Change the Progress Meeting to 10:00
4. Save the document
5. Create a Macro to Update the Table of Contents
6. Preview the results

Watermarks

A watermark is any graphic or text that appears either on top or behind existing text when the document is printed, for example "Sample Document".

Picture Watermarks

1. Open a new document
2. Select 

3. Alternatively press Alt P P W W
4. The Printed Watermark dialog box appears
5. Select Picture watermark

Figure 181

6. Choose Select Picture..., locate the picture, click Insert
7. Click Apply, choose Close
8. The watermark appears in the document
9. Preview the document to view the watermark

Creating a Text Watermark

1. Open a new document
2. Select 

3. Alternatively press Alt P P W
4. Choose the text required from the default settings

Figure 182

5. The watermark appears in the document

To Customise a Text Watermark

1. Select Page Layout, Watermark, Custom Watermark...
2. The Printed Watermark dialog box appears

Figure 183

3. Select Te**x**t watermark, click on the ▼ arrow, select the required text

Figure 184

4. Make changes to the **F**ont, **S**ize and **C**olour text layout as necessary
5. Click Apply, choose Close

To Delete a Watermark

1. Select Page Layout, Watermark, Remove Watermark

2. Alternatively press Alt P P W R
3. The Watermark is removed from the document

Exercise 16: - Creating a Watermark

1. Create a Watermark
2. Edit the Watermark
3. Preview the Watermark
4. Delete the Watermark

Hyperlinks

Hyperlinks allow users to move to a new destination by clicking with the left button for example, using hyperlinks in an electronic document such as a Table of Contents where the mouse pointer is moved over the page number relating to a topic. Hyperlinks can contain links in the same document or links to other applications, or a particular website. Hyperlinks can be assigned to text, graphics or pictures and can be created to open an existing file, web page, a place in a document, create a link to a new document or an E-mail address.

Creating a Hyperlink to an Internet Address

1. Open a new document, type Smart PC Guides
2. Click Insert, Hyperlink, alternatively press Ctrl K
3. The Insert Hyperlink dialog box appears

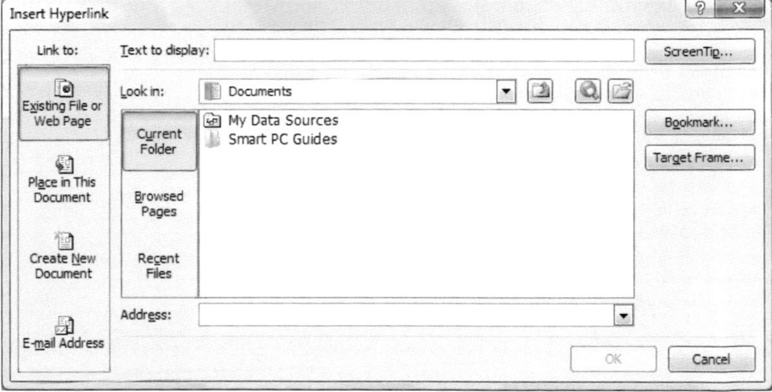

Figure 185

4. Under Link to: select Existing File or Web Page
5. In the Text to display area type Smart PC Guides
6. Select ScreenTip...

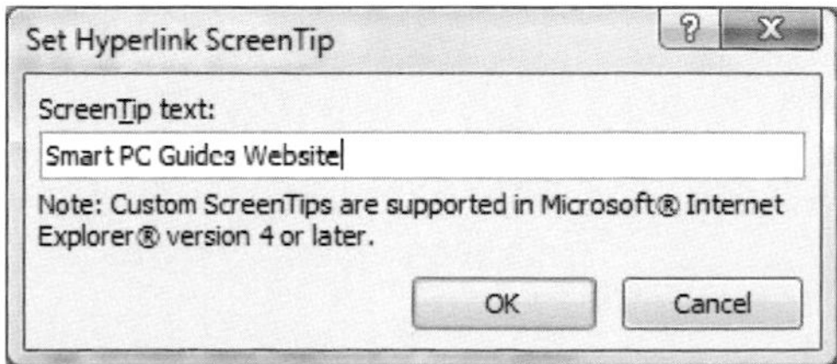

Figure 186

7. Type "Smart PC Guides Website", click OK
8. Click in the Address field

Address: http://www.smart-pc-guides.com

Figure 187

9. Type the web address http://www.smart-pc-guides.com
10. Click OK
11. The hyperlink Smart PC Guides appears in the document
12. Hold the Ctrl key down, click on the link with the left button
13. The Smart PC Guides Home Page appears
14. Press back to go back to the document

Creating a Hyperlink in a Document

1. Create a bookmark within a document, for example Chapter 1
2. Repeat the process to create bookmarks for Chapters 2 and 3
3. Select the position where you want to create a hyperlink

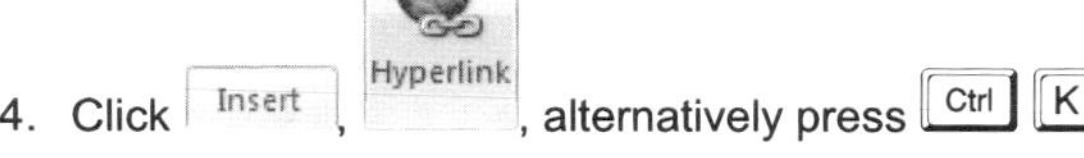

4. Click Insert, Hyperlink, alternatively press Ctrl K
5. The Insert Hyperlink dialog box appears
6. Select Place in This Document

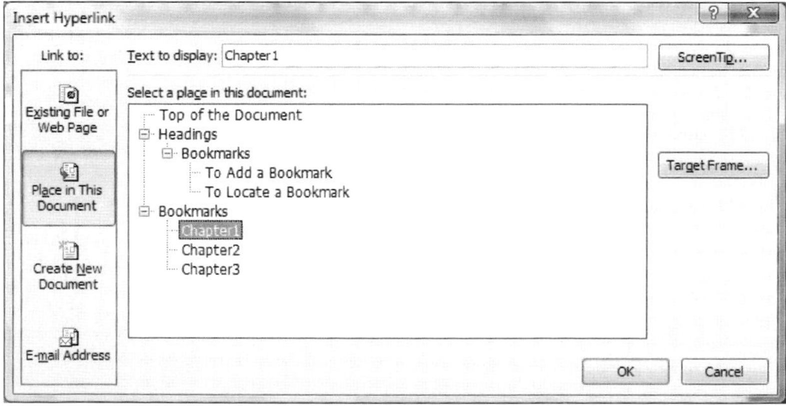

Figure 188

7. Choose the bookmark Chapter1, select OK
8. Press the Ctrl key, click on the link with the left button
9. The cursor appears before the text Chapter 1

Edit a Hyperlink

1. Press with the left button on the hyperlink
2. Click with the right button, select Edit Hyperlink...

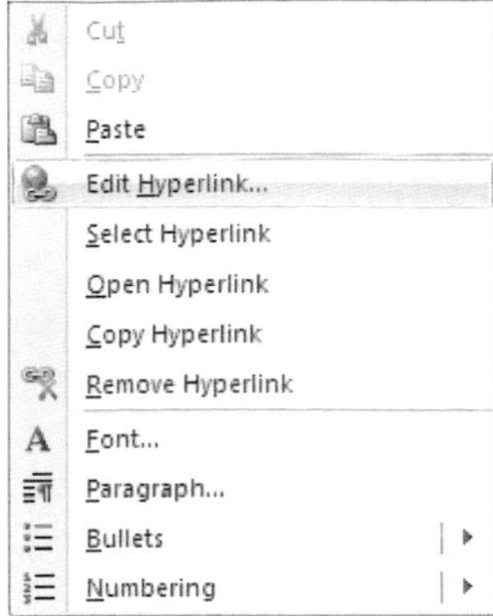

Figure 189

3. The Edit Hyperlink dialog box appears

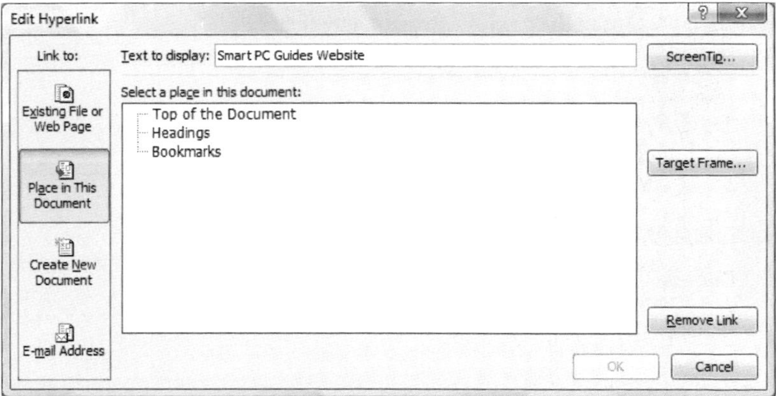

Figure 190

4. In Text to display, change the information as shown above, click OK
5. The new link is displayed as Smart PC Guides Website

Delete a Hyperlink

1. Select the Hyperlink Smart PC Guides Website
2. Click with the right button, select Remove Hyperlink
3. The text is displayed without the hyperlink

Using Format Columns Feature

1. Open a new document
2. Choose Page Layout, Breaks to expand the menu
3. Choose Continuous — Insert a section break and start the new section on the same page.
4. Alternatively press Alt I B

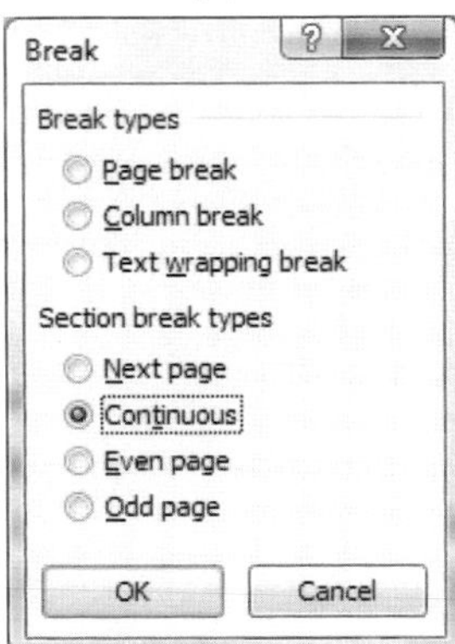

Figure 191

5. Choose Continuous, press OK
6. Select Page Layout, Columns to expand the menu
7. Choose Columns to display the Columns dialog box
8. Alternatively press Alt O C

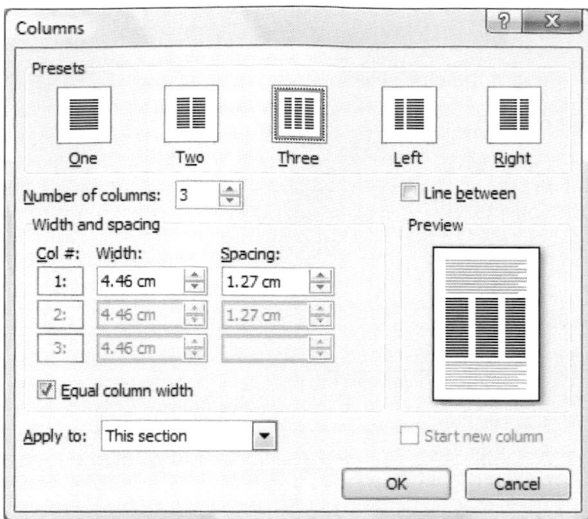

Figure 192

9. Select Presets, choose Three
10. The Preview area displays the chosen selection
11. Width and Spacing can be adjusted using the arrows
12. Select Apply to, choose This point forward, click OK
13. Type the required text or copy and paste the text
14. The text appears in the columns
15. To return to a single column, choose Page Layout, Breaks
16. Choose

17. Press Alt O C to display the Columns dialog box
18. Select One
19. Select Apply to, choose This point forward, click OK

Insert a Chart in a Document

1. Position the cursor where the chart is required
2. Select Insert, Object
3. The Object dialog box appears

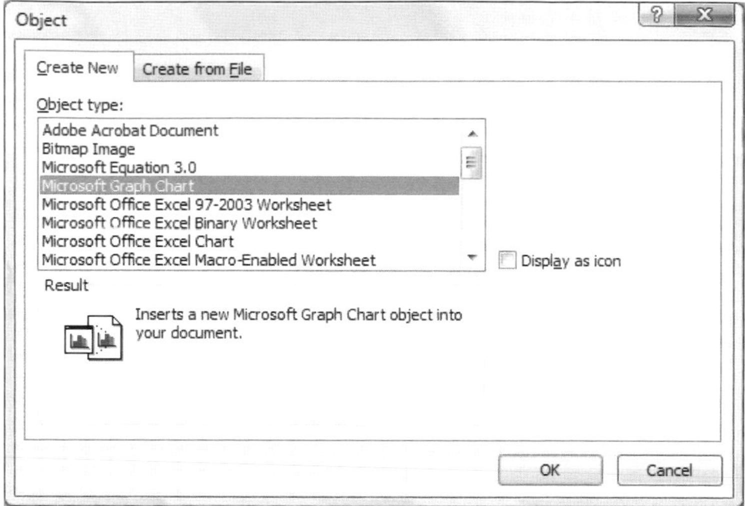

Figure 193

4. Choose **C**reate New, arrow down and select Microsoft Graph Chart
5. Click OK, the Datasheet box appears showing the default chart

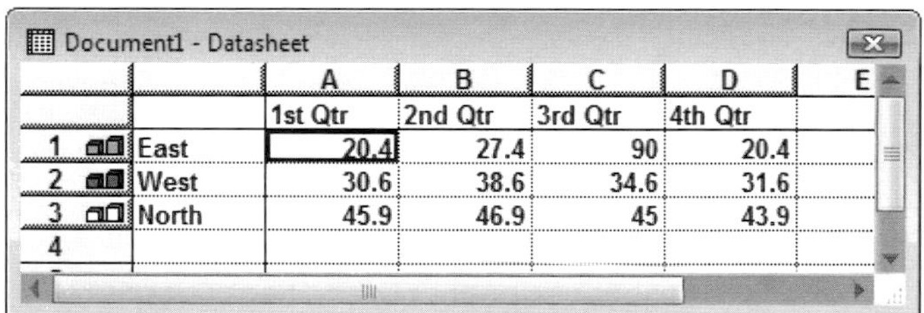
Document1 - Datasheet

		A	B	C	D	E
		1st Qtr	2nd Qtr	3rd Qtr	4th Qtr	
1	East	20.4	27.4	90	20.4	
2	West	30.6	38.6	34.6	31.6	
3	North	45.9	46.9	45	43.9	
4						

Figure 194

6. To adjust columns or rows, click on the sizing handles and drag
7. Delete the existing text in the default datasheet
8. To alter text or figures, click in a cell and type the required text
9. Click outside the document, the chart appears in the document

Edit a Chart

1. Double click the left button in the chart to bring up the datasheet
2. Amend the text as required, click outside the document
3. The amended chart is displayed in the document

Copy Information from Excel

1. Open Microsoft Excel, create the following data in a new spreadsheet

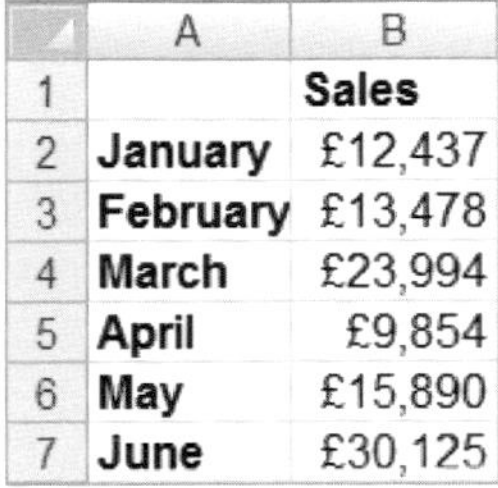

	A	B
1		**Sales**
2	**January**	£12,437
3	**February**	£13,478
4	**March**	£23,994
5	**April**	£9,854
6	**May**	£15,890
7	**June**	£30,125

Figure 195

2. Click the left button in cell A1, highlight to B7
3. Select Ctrl C
4. Switch to Microsoft Word
5. Press the left button where the data is to appear
6. Select Ctrl V to paste the information into the document

Using Edit Paste Special

1. Instead of selecting Paste when the information is copied from Excel
2. Choose 

3. Alternatively Alt Ctrl V displays the Paste Special dialog box
4. Select the option Paste link
5. Choose Microsoft Office Excel Worksheet Object

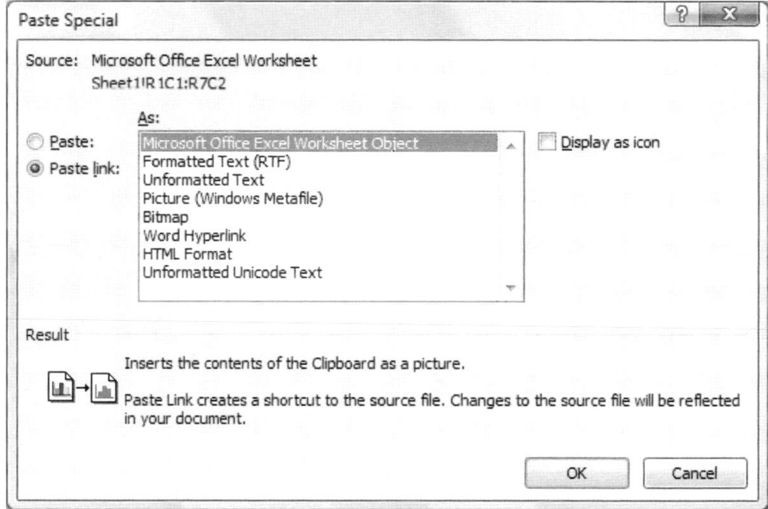

Figure 196

6. Click OK to paste the link into the document

	Sales
January	£12,437
February	£13,478
March	£23,994
April	£9,854
May	£15,890
June	£30,125

Figure 197

7. Change the information in one cell in Excel, switch back to Word
8. The Word document has been updated

Note: Make sure that the user has access to all linked information if this option is used.

Exercise 17: - Using Columns, Hyperlinks and Macros

Using 2 columns read the following text; reproduce the exercise exactly as shown in a new blank document. Save the document as Mylinks.doc

- Open up a New blank document
- Save the document
- Name the document as Mylinks.doc

1. Select Format, Columns
2. Choose a two column option
3. Create the text as shown

Open Excel

- Open up Microsoft Excel
- Select a cell of your choice
- Create the information below
- Save the spreadsheet as linking.xls
- Close the spreadsheet

Month	*Sales*
January	£12,437.00
February	£13,478.00
March	£23,994.00
April	£9,854.00
May	£15,890.00
June	£30,125.00

Inserting Excel Data

1. Select the position for insertion in Word
2. Click, Insert Object
3. Select the option, Create from File
4. Place a tick in the box, Link to File
5. Browse for the excel file required
6. Select OK
7. The data from Excel appears in Word

Note: If the link to file option is used any changes will affect the layout of this document e.g. if you created a chart in the same worksheet

Modify Linked Data

- Double click on the excel data
- Select the excel data
- Change the font size to Size 9
- Select Save in Excel
- Close Down Excel
- The data changes in the Document

Open Excel

1. Open the file in Excel named Linking
2. In the Month Column
3. Change months July to December
4. Save the Excel document

Inserting Excel Data

- Open an existing spreadsheet
- Highlight the text
- Select Ctrl C
- Switch to Microsoft Word
- Press Alt Ctrl V to view Paste Special
- Select Paste the source as a picture
- Click OK
- The results appear in Word

Create a Macro

Create macro named **AutoExec** assign this to a document. The macro should go into preview upon opening. Create a second macro assigned to the same document only using the shortcut key ALT and E to close the document.

Using Hyperlinks in PowerPoint

Staff that deliver presentations might consider using hyperlinks, the benefit being that when delivering a presentation a hyperlink could enable the audience to view statistical information in either Word or Excel.

- Create a hyperlink
- Leave the text to display field blank
- Locate the required file
- Click on the OK icon

When running the slide show

- Move the mouse pointer over the slide
- Click with the left mouse button
- The file opens

To return back to the presentation, select ALT and E from the macro that was created in Word to close the file and returns the person back to the PowerPoint presentation.

Working with Graphics

Documents can be enhanced and made more interesting by inserting graphics, drawing objects, pictures, charts or text. A Bitmap picture made up from a series of small dots that form shapes and lines cannot be converted to drawing objects or ungrouped but can be scaled, cropped and re-coloured. Pictures made up as metafiles (most ClipArt) can be ungrouped.

Inserting a Picture in a Document

1. Open a document where a picture is required
2. Place the cursor at the point where the picture is to be inserted

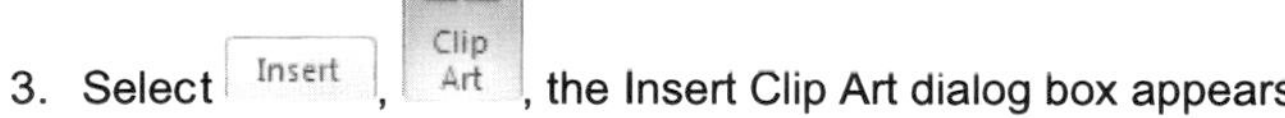

3. Select Insert, Clip Art, the Insert Clip Art dialog box appears

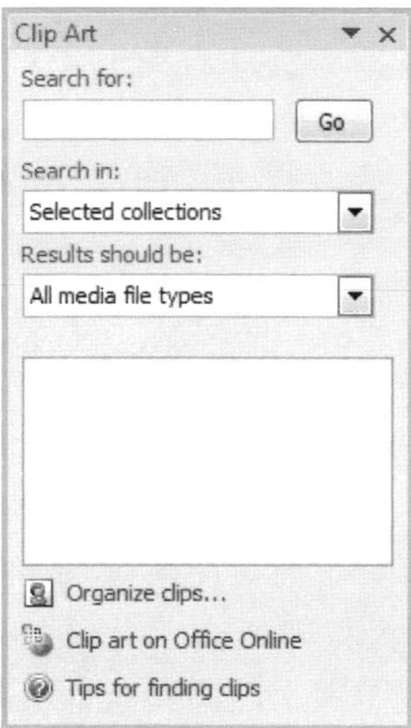

Figure 198

4. In the Search for: box type, Business, press Go
5. The Insert Clip Art dialog box shows the results
6. Click on the arrow on the picture, select Insert

Figure 199

7. The picture is displayed in the document
8. To delete the picture, click in the picture with the left button, press Delete

Edit a Picture in a Document

1. Open a document that contains text and a picture
2. Click on the picture

Figure 200

3. Move the mouse pointer over the sizing handles
4. Drag to edit the picture
5. To move the picture to another position, click in the picture and drag
6. To rotate the picture, click in the picture, the Picture Tools Tab appears
7. Select Rotate from the Format Arrange Grouping
8. Move the mouse pointer over the options to show how the picture looks

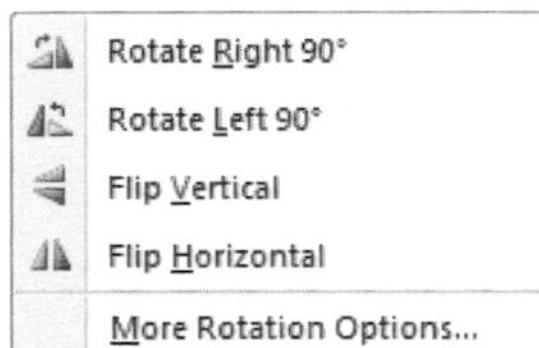

Figure 201

9. Select Flip Horizontal
10. Move the mouse pointer to a green circle, a black circular arrow appears
11. Click and hold down the left button drag to rotate to the required position

Figure 202

Cropping Pictures

The Picture Tools option appears when a picture is selected in a document.

1. Click the left button on the Format Tab to display the Picture Tools
2. Select a picture by using the left button

Figure 203

3. Click the Crop icon 

from the Picture Tools

Figure 204

4. Move over a black handle
5. Drag over the area that needs to be taken out
6. Repeat the process until you see the tigers face

Figure 205

7. Press the left button and drag to hide the information not required
8. Select Size from the Picture Tools

Figure 206

9. Click the arrows in the height and width area to increase or decrease the size
10. Expand the Size Grouping by clicking on
11. The Size dialog box appears

12. Alternatively select the picture to be resized
13. Right click on the picture select Size...

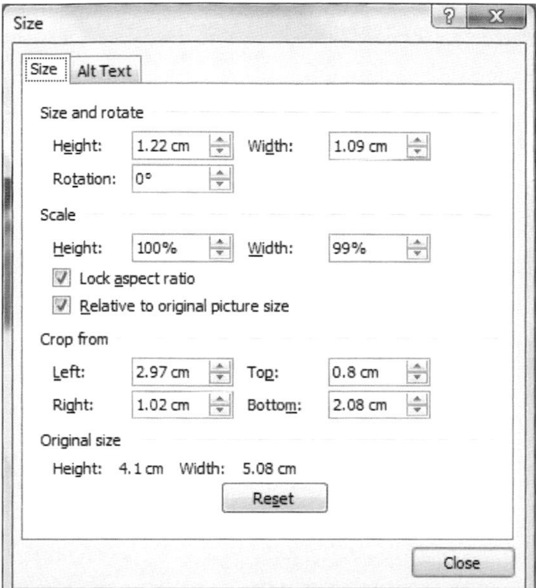

Figure 207

14. In the Scale area, amend the **<u>H</u>**eight and **<u>W</u>**idth to 300%
15. Click Close

Inserting WordArt into a Document

1. To insert text as an object, select Insert, 

2. The WordArt Gallery appears

Figure 208

3. Select a style, the Edit WordArt dialog box appears

Figure 209

4. Select the Font and Size required
5. In the Text box type ABC Limited, click OK
6. The text appears in the document

Figure 210

7. Click on 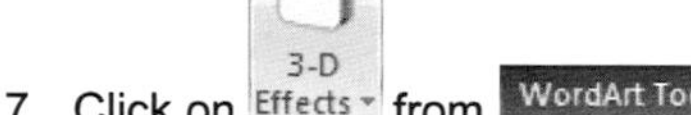 3-D Effects from WordArt Tools
8. Select 3-D Parallel Style 

Figure 211

9. To rotate text select the appropriate option 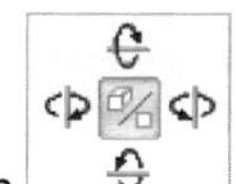 from 3-D Effects
10. To add lighting to the text
11. Select 3-D Effects, 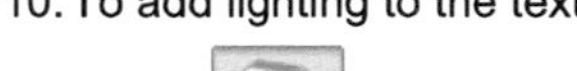 Lighting
12. Choose the angle of lighting required 

To add a shadow

1. Select 

2. Choose Shadow Style 1

Figure 212

Edit WordArt in a Document

1. Right click on the text to be edited
2. Select Edit Text...
3. The Edit WordArt dialog box appears
4. Edit text as required, click OK

Format WordArt in a Document

1. To change the colour of the WordArt, click on the text to be changed

Figure 213

2. Select WordArt Tools, click on Shape Fill choose the required colour

Figure 214

3. To format the WordArt, click in the WordArt to be changed
4. Click with the right button, select Format WordArt...
5. The Format WordArt dialog box appears

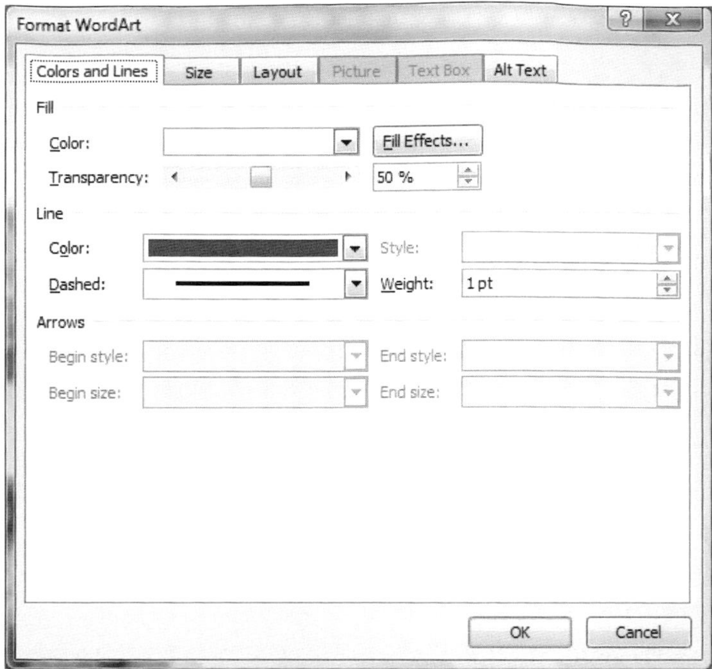

Figure 215

6. Select the Colours and Lines Tab, change the line colour
7. To alter the size, select the Size Tab, make any adjustments
8. To alter the layout, select the Layout Tab, click on the layout required
9. Press OK

Adding AutoShapes to Documents

Ready made basic shapes for example, rectangles, circles, block arrows, flowcharts, symbols, banners and callouts can be added to documents to enhance its appearance.

1. Select Insert, Shapes from the Illustrations grouping
2. The Shapes gallery appears, choose Callouts

Figure 216

3. Select a shape

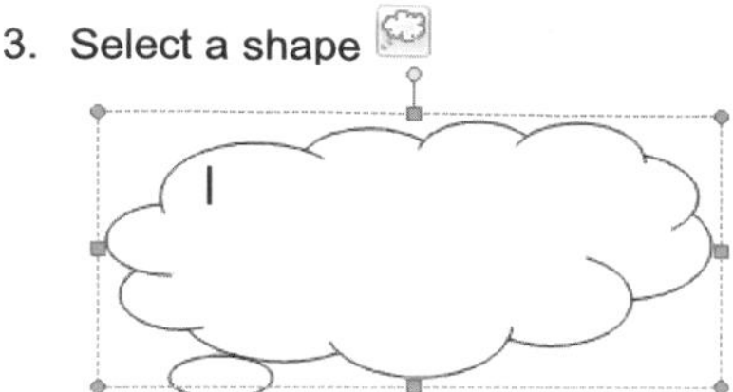

Figure 217

4. Drag in the document for the AutoShape to appear
5. Type in the AutoShape the text required
6. The text appears in the AutoShape in the document

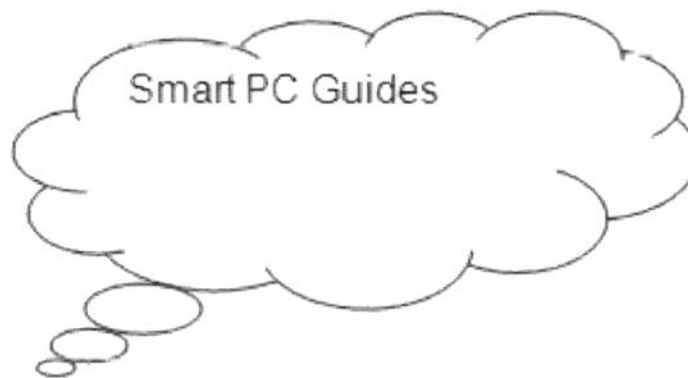

Figure 218

Using the Drawing Toolbar

1. To use a drawing object, select Line from the Shapes gallery

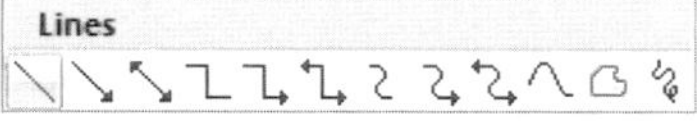

Figure 219

2. Hold down the left button and drag
3. Click back on the Line icon
4. Position the mouse pointer on the circle next to the line and drag

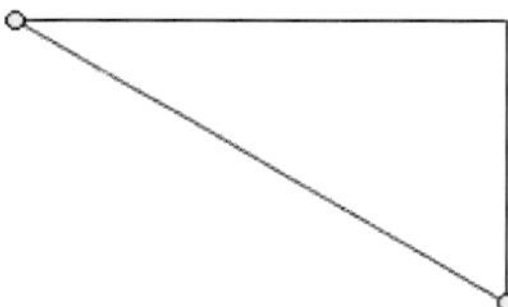

Figure 220

5. Repeat the above steps to complete the required shape

6. To draw a shape, click on the shape from the Shapes gallery
7. Move the mouse pointer where you want the object to appear
8. Hold down the left button and drag, release the mouse button
9. Repeat the process to create as many shapes as required

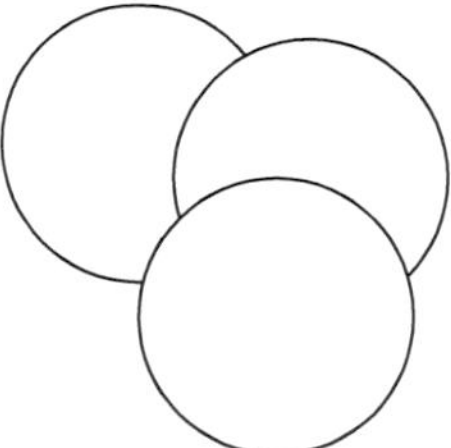

Figure 221

To Draw Objects from a Central Point

1. Click in the document where the object is to appear
2. Select an object from the Shapes gallery using the left button
3. Press and hold down the Ctrl key and drag the object onto the page
4. Release the mouse button before the Ctrl key
5. Click outside the drawing box

Figure 222

6. To add a 3-D effect, select the object
7. Select Format from the Drawing Tools
8. Click on the 3-D Effects icon 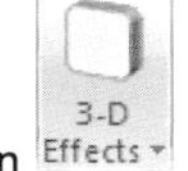

Figure 223

Using Text Boxes

Text boxes allow text to be positioned anywhere in a document.

1. To insert a text box, select Insert, Text Box

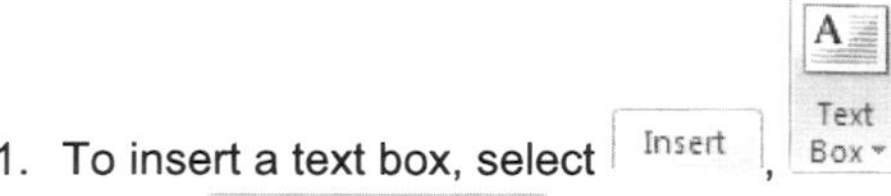

2. Select Draw Text Box
3. Click where you want to start the text box, drag to the required size

Figure 224

4. Type inside the box to add text
5. To move the text box, click on the edge of the box
6. Use the arrow keys ↓ ↑ → ← to move the text box to the new position
7. Alternatively click with the left button on the edge of the text box and drag
8. Release the mouse when the text box is in its new location
9. To delete a box, position the mouse pointer over the edge of the text box
10. A four headed arrow appears, click on the border, press Delete

To Link a Text Box

Linking allows text to flow from one text box to another.

1. Open the text boxes where text is to flow from
2. Right click on the border of the first text box
3. Choose Create Text Box Link
4. Position the cursor over the second text box
5. Click with the left button the Mug pointer is displayed with an arrow
6. Type the text in the first box
7. The text automatically flows into the second text box

Display Text Box Tools

When a text box is selected, text box tools is displayed enabling the user to change features using Groups and Commands that relate to drawing, changing text direction, creating and breaking linked text boxes, text box styles, shadow effects, 3D effects, arranging and positioning text boxes and changing the size of text boxes.

To use Text Wrapping

Text can be forced to wrap around objects in a document.

1. Open a new document
2. Type the text shown below

   By moving the wrap points the text wraps around the butterfly so that the butterfly sits nicely inside the text and so becomes part of the text

   Figure 225
3. Select a place in the text where the picture is to appear
4. Choose Insert, Shapes, New Drawing Canvas

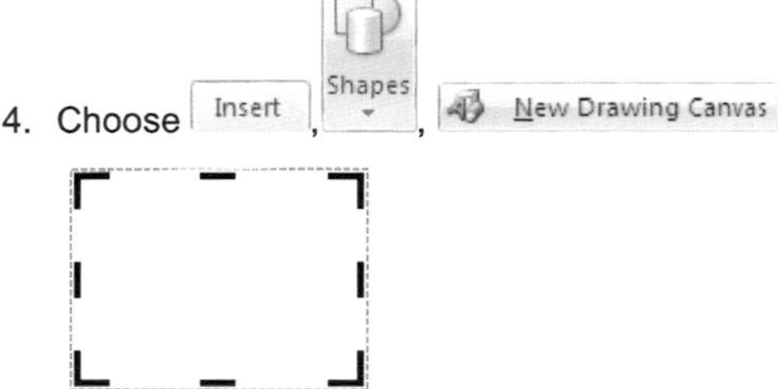

Figure 226

5. Click on any of the corner black square handles, drag to the required size
6. Click in the box, select Insert, Clip Art
7. The Clip Art dialog box appears

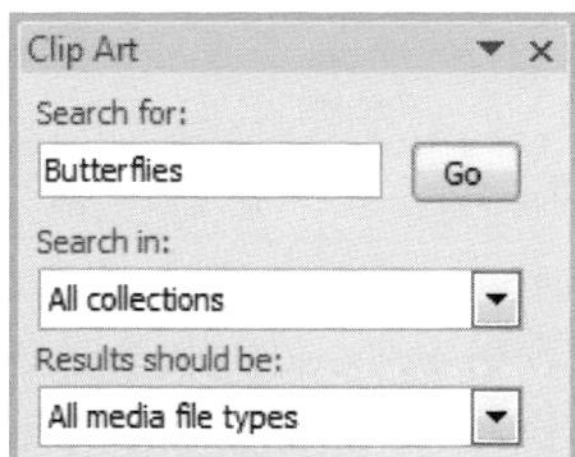

Figure 227

8. In the Search for: box type Butterflies, press Go
9. The Clip Art dialog box shows the results

10. Click on the picture to insert it into the drawing canvas

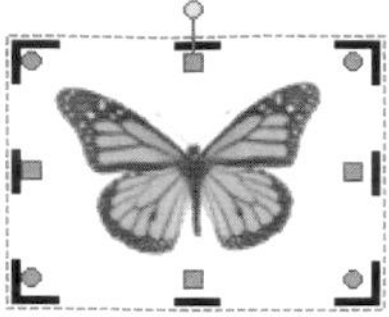

Figure 228

11. Click outside the picture on the blue dotted line
12. Select Format from the Drawing Tools
13. Choose Text Wrapping, Edit Wrap Points
14. The picture appears as shown below

Figure 229

15. Click on the black squares and drag to the required position
16. The text appears around the picture

By moving the wrap points the butterfly sits nicely inside  the text wraps around the butterfly so that the text and so becomes part of the text.

Figure 230

Using Footnotes and Endnotes

A footnote explains what text is in a document and is placed at the foot of a page. If it is placed at the end of the document it is known as an Endnote. Footnotes and Endnotes consist of two parts, the note reference mark that is characterised by a number or character within the body of the text referring to additional text in a footnote, and the note text that contains the descriptive text.

Inserting a Footnote

1. Position the pointer in the text where the footnote reference mark is to appear
2. Select, 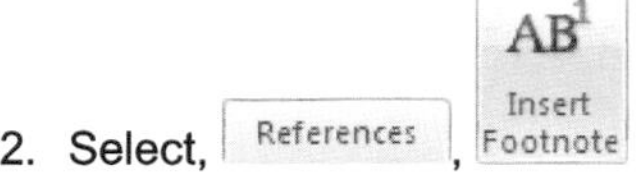

3. The following prompt appears at the foot of the page

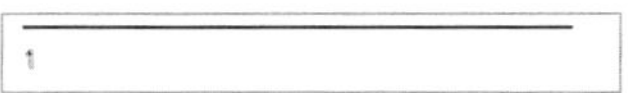

Figure 231

4. Type the text required for the footnote
5. The following prompt appears in the document to indicate a footnote [1]

A footnote explains what text is in a document and is placed at the foot of a page. If it is placed at the end of the document it is known as an Endnote. [1]Footnotes and Endnotes consist of two parts, the note reference mark that is characterised by a number or character within the body of the text referring to additional text in a footnote, and the note text that contains the descriptive text.

Figure 232

6. The note text appears at the bottom of the page

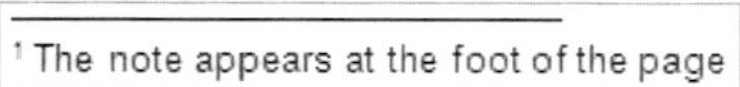

Figure 233

Inserting a Endnote

Follow the steps for Footnote, select Insert Endnote

1. The endnote reference mark appears in the text identified by an [i]
2. The endnote appears at the end of the document

[i] This endnote appears at the end of the document

Figure 234

To Amend a Footnote or Endnote

1. Place the mouse pointer over the footnote or endnote reference mark in the text
2. Double click with the left button
3. The cursor appears at the end of the page, amend text as necessary
4. Click with the left button to take you back to the document

To Delete a Footnote or Endnote

Place the mouse pointer over the footnote or endnote reference mark in the text, press Delete.

To Start Renumbering a Footnote or Endnote

1. Select References, click on the downward pointing arrow from the Footnotes grouping

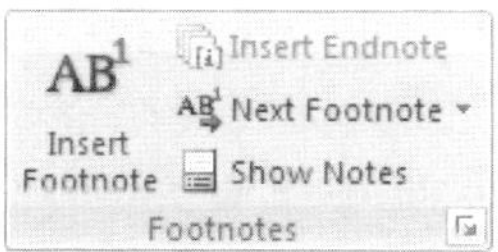

Figure 235

2. The Footnote and Endnote dialog appears

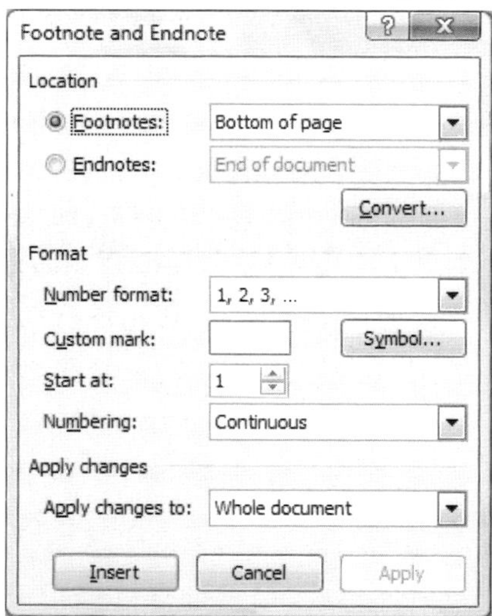

Figure 236

3. Select Footnotes, choose Numbering
4. Click Restart each page, press Apply

Shortcut Keys

SHORTCUT KEYS	DESCRIPTION	SHORTCUT KEYS	DESCRIPTION
Ctrl F1	Hide or Display the Ribbon	F1	Word Help
Ctrl F2	Displays Print Preview	F5	Display Go To Dialog Box
Ctrl A	Highlights Whole Document	F7	Spell Checker
Ctrl B	Apply or Remove Bold Format	F10	Display/Hide Shortcut Keys
Ctrl C	Copy Text	F12	Displays Save As Dialog Box
Ctrl D	Displays Font Dialog Box	Alt F I A	Word Advanced Options
Ctrl E	Centre Alignment Option	Alt F I P	Displays AutoCorrect Icon
Ctrl F	Displays Find and Replace Box	Alt I B	Insert Break Dialog Box
Ctrl G	Displays Go To Dialog Box	Alt N K	Bookmark Dialog Box
Ctrl H	Displays Find and Replace Box	Alt N T D	Displays the Drawing Tool
Ctrl I	Apply or Remove Text in Italic	Alt O T	Hide/Show Tabs Dialog Box
Ctrl J	Apply or Remove Justification	Alt P P W W	Watermark Dialog Box
Ctrl K	Inserts Hyperlink Dialog Box	Alt P P W	Displays Watermark
Ctrl L	Aligns Text to the Left	Alt P P W R	Removes Watermark
Ctrl N	Inserts New Document	Alt S T I	Table of Contents Dialog Box
Ctrl O	Displays Open Dialog Box	Alt W E	Displays Draft View
Ctrl P	Displays Print Dialog Box	Alt W F	Displays Full Reading View
Ctrl R	Align Text to Right	Alt W L	Displays Web Layout View
Ctrl S	Saves the Document	Alt W M R	Record New Macro Dialog
Ctrl U	Apply or Remove Underline	Alt W P	Displays Print Layout View
Ctrl V	Paste Information	Alt W R	Displays/Hide Ruler
Ctrl X	Cuts Information	Alt F8	Displays Macros
Ctrl Y	Redo Feature	Shift F3	Apply Caps/Lower/Title Case
Ctrl Z	Undo Feature	Shift F7	Displays Thesaurus Feature

This concludes the Word 2007 Foundation to Expert Guide. Thank you for choosing Smart PC Guides. To see the complete range of Smart PC Guides please visit our website www.smart-pc-guides.com

Notes Pages

Index

AutoCorrect Facility
- Deleting an AutoCorrect Entry 32
- Opening the AutoCorrect Facility........30

AutoSummarise
- Altering the Display of a Document.....90
- Creating a Summary or Abstract.........90
- Displaying and Highlighting Key Points in a Document.................................90
- Reading a Summary of an Online Document.......................................89

AutoText Entries...................................136
- Creating Date Fields..........................138
- Using the ASK Field..........................140
- Using the AutoText List.....................139

Bookmarks
- Adding a Bookmark.............................81
- Deleting a Bookmark...........................83
- Locating a Bookmark..........................82

Breaks
- Creating a Section Break 63
- Deleting Breaks..................................66

Bullets and Numbering
- Continue a Numbered List 46
- Creating a Bulleted List as you Type..44
- Creating a Bulleted List from the Bullet Library...44
- Creating a Numbered List...................46
- Creating your own Numbering Style...47
- Customising a Bulleted List.................45
- Restarting Numbering 46

Charts
- Edit a Chart.......................................161
- Inserting a Chart In a Document.......160

Comments
- Deleting a Comment...........................93
- Editing a Comment.............................92
- Inserting a Comment..........................92
- Viewing Comments 93

Comparing Multiple Documents 93

Copying Information
- Using Keyboard Shortcuts to Copy Information 25
- Using the Mouse Pointer to Drag and Copy Information............................25
- Using the Mouse to Copy Information.25

Copying Information from Excel 161

Copying Information in a Document........25

Creating an Outlined Numbered List.....123

Creating and Saving a Document...........14

Drives, Folders and Files
- Creating a Folder................................14
- Creating a Sub-Folder.........................14
- How Information is Stored..................13
- My Documents 13

Edit Paste Special................................ 162

Endnotes and Footnotes
- Amending Footnotes or Endnotes.... 178
- Deleting a Footnote or Endnote........ 178
- Inserting a Endnote........................... 177
- Inserting Footnotes 177
- Renumbering a Footnote or Endnote 178

Exercise 01
- Creating and Saving a Document in Word 17

Exercise 02
- Using the Copy and Move Functions . 26

Exercise 03
- Using Smart Tags to Add an Address 29

Exercise 04
- Bulleted Lists...................................... 48

Exercise 05
- Creating a Simple Table 54

Exercise 06
- Creating a Booking Form................... 62

Exercise 07
- Creating a Header and Footer 67

Exercise 08
- Creating Tabs using the Tabs Dialog Box.. 71

Exercise 09
- Creating a Document using Styles 80

Exercise 10
- Updating a Table of Contents............ 85

Exercise 11
- Creating Labels................................ 113

Exercise 12
- Working with a Table of Contents..... 122

Exercise 13
- Creating a Form using the Form Commands 128

Exercise 14
- Using Fill-in Fields 142

Exercise 15
- Generating a Table of Contents Macro 150

Exercise 16
- Creating a Watermark....................... 154

Exercise 17
- Using Columns, Hyperlinks and Macros 163

Exert Level Objectives 118

Format Columns Feature 158

Format Options
- Formating using the Font Group......... 33
- Formatting using the Menu Options ... 34
- Formatting using the Paragrah Group 35
- Keep Lines Together 38
- Keep with Next Option 38

Page Break Before 38
Suppress Line Numbers 38
Text Wrap 38
The Font Group Icons 32
The Paragraph Group Icons 35
Window/Orphan Control 37
Format Painter 38
Forms
Customising the Check Box Form Fields 132
Customising the Text Form Fields 130
Inserting Check Box Form Fields 129
Inserting Text Form Fields 129
Protecting Forms 134
Foundation Level Objectives 9
Graphics
Adding a Shadow 170
Adding AutoShapes to Documents 171
Cropping Pictures 166
Drawing Objects from a Central Point 173
Edit a Picture in a Document 165
Editing WordArt in a Document 170
Formatting WordArt in a Document 170
Inserting a Picture in a Document 164
Inserting WordArt into a Document 168
Linking Text Boxes 174
Using Text Boxes 174
Using Text Wrapping 175
Using the Drawing Toolbar 172
Hard Spacing
Creating a Hard Space 30
Header and Footer
Creating Information in the Header and Footer 39
Moving between sections of a Document 66
Highlighting Information in a Document
Highlighting a Character, Word, Sentence, Paragraph or Whole Document 23
Hyperlinks
Creating a Hyperlink in a Document 156
Creating a Hyperlink to an Internet Address 155
Deleting a Hyperlink 157
Edit a Hyperlink 157
Index 181
Indexes
Creating an Index 86
Intermediate Level Objectives 55
Introducing the Word Screen 10
Commands 11
Core Tasks 11
Draft View 12
Full Screen Reading View 12
Groups 11
Help 11
Office Button 10
Outline View 12
Print Layout View 12
Quick Access Toolbar 10
Ruler 11
Scroll Bars 11
Status Bar 12
The Ribbon 11
Title Bar 11
Web Layout View 12
Zoom Control 11
Macros
Assigning a Macro to a Shortcut Key 146
Deleting a Macro 149
Recording a Macro 144
Using the Menu Bar to View and Edit a Macro 147
Mail Merge
Creating Labels 106
Creating Letters 96
Master Documents
Creating a Master Document 124
Deleting a Subdocument 127
Inserting a Subdocument 125
Lock and Unlock Subdocuments 127
Moving a Subdocument 126
Opening a Subdocument 125
Moving Information
Using Keyboard Shortcuts to Move Information 24
Using the Mouse Pointer to Move, Drag and Drop Information 24
Using the Mouse to Move Information 24
Notes Page 118
Notes Pages 180
Opening Documents
Amending or Deleting recently used Files 20
Office Button 18
Open Several Documents using the Shift Key 19
Opening Documents using the Mouse 18
Opening Several Documents using the Control Key 19
Opening Word 13
Outline View 119
Page Setup
Page Setup Group 40
Print Preview 42
Printing a Document 43
Shortcut Keys 32, 35, 179
Smart Tags 27
Removing Smart Tags 28
Spell and Grammar Facility 21
Adding Words to the Dictionary 22
Grammar Check Facility 22

Styles
- Adding a Style to a Template.............75
- Assigning a Shortcut Key to a New Style 76
- Creating a New Style..........................75
- Deleting a Style already added to a Template 78
- How to View Styles in a Document.....72
- Modifying Styles 73
- The Automatic Update Feature...........75
- Working with Styles using the Formatting Toolbar..........................73

Tab Stop Marker.....................................68
- Different Tab and Ident Icons..............68
- Removing Tabs from the Ruler...........69
- Seting Tabs using the Tab Dialog Box69
- Setting Tabs from the Ruler................68

Table of Contents.......................................4
- Creating a Table of Contents..............83

Tables
- Creating a Table using the Drawing Pencil...59
- Creating a Table using the Insert Table Feature..52
- Creating a Table using the Table Grouping Command........................49
- Creating Columns 50
- Deleting a Table Style.........................59
- Deleting Columns 51
- Deleting Rows....................................51
- Inserting Rows 50
- Merging or Joining Cells 51
- Rotating Text in a Table......................60
- Using the AutoFit Feature..................56

Templates
- Opening and Amending an existing Document 116
- Saving a Document as a Template .. 114

The Paper Tab 41

Track Changes
- How to use Track Changes 91

Undo and Redo Facility............................ 22

Using the Outline View
- Moving Information in Outline View .. 121
- Outlining an Existing Document 119
- Promote and Demote Information 120

Watermarks
- Creating a Text Watermark 152
- Customising a Text Watermark 152
- Deleting a Watermark 153
- Picture Watermarks 151